HEAD SCRATCHERS

WHEN THE WORDS OF JESUS DON'T MAKE SENSE

HEAD SCRATCHERS

WHEN THE WORDS OF JESUS
DON'T MAKE SENSE

TALBOT DAVIS

HEAD SCRATCHERS
WHEN THE WORDS OF JESUS DON'T MAKE SENSE
Copyright © 2015 by Abingdon Press

This book is printed on acid-free paper.

Scripture quotations unless noted otherwise are from the Common English Bible. Copyright © 2011 by the Common English Bible. All rights reserved. Used by permission. *www.CommonEnglishBible.com.*

Scripture quotations marked (NIV) are taken from the Holy Bible, New International Version®, NIV®. Copyright © 1973, 1978, 1984, 2011 by Biblica, Inc.™ Used by permission of Zondervan. All rights reserved worldwide. *www.zondervan.com.* The "NIV" and "New International Version" are trademarks registered in the United States Patent and Trademark Office by Biblica, Inc.™

Scripture quotations taken from the New American Standard Bible®, Copyright © 1960, 1962, 1963, 1968, 1971, 1972, 1973, 1975, 1977, 1995 by The Lockman Foundation. Used by permission. (*www.Lockman.org*)

Scripture quotations noted KJV are from the King James Version of the Bible.

Scripture quotations noted Douay-Rheims Version are from the Douay-Rheims Catholic Bible.

Al Web addresses were correct and operational at time of publication.

Library of Congress Cataloging-in-Publication Data

Davis, Talbot.
 Head scratchers : when the words of Jesus don't make sense / Talbot Davis. -- First [edition].
   pages cm
  ISBN 978-1-5018-0288-1 (binding: soft back)
 1. Jesus Christ--Teachings I. Title.
 BS2415.D385 2015
 226'.06--dc23

                                         2015005958

15 16 17 18 19 20 21 22 23 24—10 9 8 7 6 5 4 3 2 1
MANUFACTURED IN THE UNITED STATES OF AMERICA

CONTENTS

Audio recordings of Davis's Head Scratchers sermons may be downloaded for free at the following website, as another way for you to experience each chapter.

Abingdonpress.com/TalbotDavis

INTRODUCTION

When Jesus Makes You Scratch Your Head

Jesus said . . . well, Jesus said all kinds of things, didn't he?

Many of them were *comforting*, like "My yoke is easy to bear, and my burden is light."

Others of them were *inspiring*, as in "I came so that they could have life—indeed, so that they could live life to the fullest."

Some of them were *liberating*, communicating both the depths of our need and the heights of God's kingdom: "Then you will know the truth, and the truth will set you free."

But other times, Jesus said things that were . . . *perplexing*. *Confusing*. Even *insulting*. Or for the purposes of our time together, *head scratching*.

Why on earth would the Savior of the world say things like . . .

> *The kingdom of heaven suffers violence and the violent bear it away;*

> *Hate your father and mother;*

> *The gates of Hades will not overcome it;*

> *Whoever insults the Holy Spirit will never be forgiven;*

> and *Let the dead bury their own dead . . . ?*

Why would Jesus say these things to followers, would-be followers, opponents, and innocent bystanders? What was he trying to accomplish? How in the world can we make sense of that which appears to be both so odd and so *at odds* with the Jesus many of us have come to know and love?

Those are the questions we will wrestle with in the rest of this volume. As I prepared and delivered these messages to a real congregation in real time (more on that in a moment), I tried to keep three realities at the center of my thinking and my preaching:

1. The "Jesus many of us have come to know and love" is quite often the sanitized Jesus. And the sanitized Jesus is much less interesting, altogether less invasive than the true Jesus. When we "clean Jesus up," he becomes all about improving our lives. He's an accessory to a life we imagine we've got figured out pretty much on our own. The head scratchers, however, come from an *unfiltered* Jesus. The unfiltered Jesus is much less interested in improving our lives and much more interested in ending them. Ending them so that we may in fact be *born again*.

2. The words of the Bible in general and Jesus in particular should never be separated from the context in which they appear. While in seminary, I learned some initials that I have eagerly passed on to the people of Good Shepherd United Methodist Church: C.I.E.—Context Is Everything. In the five chapters that follow, you will see that I invariably move from the ground floor—Jesus' head scratching saying—to the thirty-thousand-foot view—the context in which he said it. *Where was he speaking? To whom? What's going on in the larger narrative of the biblical author?*

3. As we say at Good Shepherd: *The Bible is not a book. It's a library.* Unlike most libraries, however, the Bible only has one subject in its biography section: Jesus himself. So four very different authors, Matthew, Mark, Luke, and John, weigh in on this incomparable subject. Through each chapter of this study, we'll try to answer: *How does the head scratcher fit in not only with what Jesus is trying to accomplish but with what each Gospel writer has as his goals?*

As I indicated above, these chapters come from a series of sermons delivered in real time to a real congregation full of people with real issues. Good Shepherd United Methodist Church (*www.gsumc.org*) in Charlotte, North Carolina, where I have pastored since 1999, is a remarkable collection of generations, cultures, languages, and even faith commitments all operating under the banner of *inviting all people into a living relationship with Jesus Christ.* For that reason, some of the urgency you'll read on these pages comes from the all-too-real situations in which the people of the church and community find themselves.

In my experience, Jesus' ancient words—be they comforting, inspiring, or head scratching—have an uncanny ability to intersect with people's modern lives. I think that's why some folks respond to his words and even these messages with a mixture of skepticism and apathy. They say, "not for me" or "not now." And that's when the head scratching becomes heartbreaking.

But in far more cases, I have seen the opposite happen. People recognize that Jesus unfiltered is much more worthy of our surrender than Jesus sanitized, and they align their lives accordingly. They cast off that which hinders and put on that which liberates. Change of this kind is neither easy nor convenient, but it is always worth it.

That's why my prayer for these words is that they would not be a source of mere speculation and conversation, but that they would instead be instruments of transformation.

In other words, I offer you this study so that the *head scratching* will become *life changing.*

May it be so.

Talbot Davis

1

THE VIOLENT
BEAR IT AWAY

From the days of John the Baptist until now the kingdom of heaven is violently attacked as violent people seize it. (Matthew 11:12)

O f all the head scratchers we're going to be looking at together in this book, we are starting out with what for my money is the head scratcheriest of them all, Matthew 11:12. Now what makes this verse such a head scratcher is that it is so difficult to translate—there is some uncertainty as to what it really says. Let me show you what I mean: As you may or may not know, Jesus spoke in a language called Aramaic, which has a lot in common with Hebrew. And the Gospel writers wrote down Jesus' words (along with the rest of their Gospels) in a different language, Greek. And here we are, two thousand years later, reading it in English. So, of course, Jesus' words have been translated so that we can read them. And sometimes—not always, but sometimes—it can be tricky to figure out how best to translate Jesus' words. This verse, Matthew 11:12, is one of those times.

Just look at some of the ways it has been translated in different English versions:

> From the days of John the Baptist until now the kingdom of heaven is violently attacked as violent people seize it (Common English Bible).

> From the days of John the Baptist until now, the kingdom of heaven has been subjected to violence, and violent people have been raiding it (New International Version).

> From the days of John the Baptist until now, the kingdom of heaven has been forcefully advancing, and violent people have been raiding it (New International Version, alternate reading).

> From the days of John the Baptist until now the kingdom of heaven suffers violence, and violent men take it by force (New American Standard Version).

> From the days of John the Baptist until now the kingdom of heaven is forcibly entered, and violent men seize it for themselves (New American Standard Version, alternate reading).

> And from the days of John the Baptist until now, the kingdom of heaven suffereth violence, and the violent bear it away (Douay-Rheims Version).

In some translations, the kingdom of heaven is "violently attacked" (CEB) or "subjected to violence" (NIV). In others, the kingdom of heaven is "forcefully advancing" (NIV alternate reading) or "forcibly entered" (NASB, alternate reading). Not exactly two different versions of the same thing!

Now that last translation, the Douay-Rheims, is a Roman Catholic translation that is actually a little older than the King

James Version. And I am partial to that translation of this verse for nostalgic reasons: When I was in college, my senior thesis was on the Roman Catholic writer Flannery O'Connor, and her best-known novel was called *The Violent Bear It Away*, based on this verse. O'Connor had a reputation for creating bizarre characters who engage in incomprehensible acts, and *The Violent Bear It Away* is no exception. The central scene in that particular book is when a twelve-year-old backwoods prophet simultaneously baptizes and drowns a five-year-old boy with Down's syndrome.

A baptism. And a drowning. At the same time. The Kingdom advancing and the Kingdom under assault. Violently. A friend of the gospel acting as a foe of the gospel. That's why O'Connor settled on *The Violent Bear It Away* as the title of her novel, and perhaps that's why I have been drawn to this particular translation of Jesus' words in Matthew 11:12. O'Connor's book vividly captures the tension between the two different readings of this verse.

LOST IN TRANSLATION

Is the kingdom of heaven "violently attacked"? Or is it "forcefully advancing"? Is it the victim of violence, or is it in some sense the perpetrator of violence? Here's the dilemma that leads to all this head scratching: The Greek words can mean either one. So while we know what Matthew *wrote*, we are not quite sure what he *meant*. Which means we have a very difficult time knowing what Jesus *said*. Which makes it even more challenging to figure out what it *means* for us today.

In other words, there is more spade work than usual in getting from this particular verse to its intersection with our lives. And that goes a long way to explaining why, although I have been preaching for a quarter century, I have never touched this verse for a sermon before. I've just never known quite what to make of it. So when I decided to do this HEAD SCRATCHERS project, first as a sermon series and then as a book, I knew I needed to begin with this verse. And studying it ended up being about the head scratching-est experience I've ever gone through.

First, I decided that I would study it on my own. It would be me, my Bible, and the Holy Spirit. And of course a pen to write down all the brilliant insights. So I sat down and studied hard . . . and I got nothing. Crickets. In fact, I was so frustrated with how little I got that I was tempted to abandon the project and start a new one called *Easy To Understand Bible Verses!*

So then I decided I needed some help, and I should read what the experts had to say about it. I grabbed some books written by scholars and looked up what they had to say about Matthew 11:12. One expert said these words mean one thing while another claimed they mean the polar opposite. Not just something else—the exact opposite! And I thought, "Thanks very much for that information, you overly educated eggheads!" Again, I got nothing useful.

Finally, I called one of the world's leading experts on the Gospel of Matthew. Yes, there is such a thing as a world's leading expert on Matthew, and I happen to know him. His name is David Bauer, and he taught me at Asbury Seminary back when Ronald Reagan was still president and hair-metal bands were still in vogue. And Dr. Bauer laid out the possible interpretations of Matthew 11:12 for me. I checked the time on my phone when he started talking, and he went on for twenty minutes straight before I said another word.

He said it *could* mean that the kingdom of God will be the victim of violence.

Then he told me that it *could* mean that the kingdom of God advances through violence.

Then he told me it *could* mean that you're supposed to love Jesus aggressively.

Finally, he told me his own interpretation was the first option, that the kingdom of heaven will be the victim of violence. But he qualified that by saying, "But even then, I'm only sure I'm right by about fifty-one percent." Thanks a lot!

At this stage, I felt like reading a novel with a simultaneous drowning and baptism was child's play compared to getting this sermon ready. So I called a preacher friend, Carolyn Moore, whom I thought I'd heard preach on it. It turns out I was right, and she sent me some of her material. And while it was an excellent sermon, I certainly didn't want to pass it off as mine. I knew I needed something to connect with, some way of making this incomprehensible verse comprehensible for me. So what did I do?

I jotted my final notes for the night, felt my head spinning, and decided I'd just go to bed and sleep on it. Maybe the idea would come in the morning. So I got up that Sunday at Good Shepherd with no idea what to say and just started talking! OK, that is some exaggeration, but I really had to think on my feet and trust the Spirit to get through this one.

The verse is just so difficult to comprehend with all these odd words we Methodists never associate with the Prince of Peace: *violence, force, advance, seize, raid* . . . just one head scratch after another. And the key issue is that there are two very different ways to translate and interpret each phrase in this verse:

> From the days of John the Baptist until now, the kingdom of heaven is <u>violently attacked</u> as <u>violent people seize it</u>.

> From the days of John the Baptist until now, the kingdom of heaven has been <u>forcefully advancing</u>, and violent people <u>take it by force</u>.

Now please know that when Jesus uses the phrase "kingdom of heaven," he is not talking about the place you go after you die. He is talking about what it means for you in this life when you surrender to his reign and his rule. Now, we believe in heaven for those who die in faith, but whenever Jesus talks about the "kingdom of heaven," that is not what he has in mind. He is talking about life on earth under his rule, which he inaugurated when he lived among us.

So is this kingdom of heaven—life on earth under the reign of Jesus—the victim of violence, or does it in a sense benefit from violence? Does it suffer violence, or does it advance violently and aggressively? If the kingdom is the victim of violence, that second phrase probably means that violent people continually try to assault it: "Violent people seize it." But if the kingdom advances violently, the second phrase could mean we are supposed to fight our way into it or on behalf of it and "take it by force."

If we take the first view, where the kingdom of heaven is subjected to violence, we can make sense of certain disturbing things that happen. In 2010, the Taliban claimed responsibility for killing ten aid workers in Afghanistan, accusing them of spying and preaching Christianity. Though the workers were there to offer medical care, not to preach, they were from a Christian organization and were motivated by a desire to serve Christ and neighbor.[1] We can read that story and realize that Matthew 11:12 told us this would happen. Jesus said there that those whose lives are surrendered to his rule would always be subjected to violence.

If we take the second view, where the kingdom of heaven advances violently, it makes just a little bit of sense out of one of the most troubling and confusing periods in church history, the Crusades. In the Crusades, which took place between A.D. 1095 and 1291, Christians fought wars to conquer the Holy Land in the name of Jesus. Not only did Christians fight these wars, they had encouragement and even blessing from the church to do so. We look back at those events today and think such an idea is absurd. But when we read Matthew 11:12, we see that perhaps Christians understood this verse so literally that they thought the kingdom of heaven would advance violently in precisely this way.

To answer some of these questions, it is wise to move back from the ground level view of verse 11:12 and zoom out to the thirty-thousand-foot view, to get the bigger picture of where all this comes from. In other words, we need to scale back from a narrow focus on the immediate words and read these words in the larger setting in which they occur. When we read Scripture, I frequently remind the people of Good Shepherd to keep in mind the acronym C.I.E., which stands for Context Is Everything. If you rip a Bible verse out of its context, you rob it of its meaning. But when you read it within its context and see it in light of what comes before and after it, it is often much easier to understand. And Matthew 11:12 is one of those instances where context really is everything.

CONTEXT IS EVERYTHING.

This whole scene begins in Matthew 11:2, where Jesus' cousin and dear friend John the Baptist sends Jesus a message with an important question. Here is the full passage, from 11:2 to 11:15:

> [2] Now when John heard in prison about the things the Christ was doing, he sent word by his disciples to Jesus, asking, [3] "Are you the one who is to come, or should we look for another?"
> [4] Jesus responded, "Go, report to John what you hear and see. [5] Those who were blind are able to see. Those who were crippled are walking. People with skin diseases are cleansed. Those who were deaf now hear. Those who were dead are raised up. The poor have good news proclaimed to them. [6] Happy are those who don't stumble and fall because of me."
> [7] When John's disciples had gone, Jesus spoke to the crowds about John: "What did you go out to the wilderness to see? A stalk blowing in the wind? [8] What did you go out

to see? A man dressed up in refined clothes? Look, those who wear refined clothes are in royal palaces. ⁹ What did you go out to see? A prophet? Yes, I tell you, and more than a prophet. ¹⁰ He is the one of whom it is written: Look, I'm sending my messenger before you, who will prepare your way before you.

¹¹ "I assure you that no one who has ever been born is greater than John the Baptist. Yet whoever is least in the kingdom of heaven is greater than he. ¹² From the days of John the Baptist until now the kingdom of heaven is violently attacked as violent people seize it. ¹³ All the Prophets and the Law prophesied until John came. ¹⁴ If you are willing to accept it, he is Elijah who is to come. ¹⁵ Let the person who has ears, hear.

Right away, we read that John the Baptist was in prison (verse 2). Later, Matthew tells us why: He had protested against King Herod's marriage to Herodias, who had been married to Herod's brother and was, therefore, his sister-in-law (Matthew 14:3-4). This is a public stand for which John is ultimately executed (14:5-12). In Chapter 11, he is in prison awaiting his fate. The passage begins in prison, which eventually leads to execution. Violence. When we recognize the context, we see that violence is present in this passage from the outset. John was the first person to announce the kingdom of heaven, preaching, "Change your hearts and lives! Here comes the kingdom of heaven!" (Matthew 3:1-2). And now he is in prison. The Kingdom is already suffering violence.

And something about that violence, that prison experience, seems to have robbed John of some of his boldness and faith. His imprisonment must have made doubt creep into John's mind. In 11:3, we see him ask Jesus, "Are you the one who is to come, or should we look for another?" You can almost hear the pain in that question. John is there in prison, knowing his own days are probably numbered. So he sends his disciples to Jesus to ask, Are you really the one? Are you really the savior? And if so, why have you not delivered me from this prison? Are you it, or should we wait for someone better?

We wrestle with that same question even today. Some of you reading this have prayed to Jesus, have followed Jesus boldly, have put your trust in Jesus, and things still went wrong. That marriage still fell apart. That loved one still died. That compulsion still won't go away. That job still hasn't arrived. Or one of a thousand other possible misfortunes. You ask whether Jesus is really the one you should be following, or whether you ought to look for someone better. At some point we all ask: Is there someone else out there who can deliver me from who I am or what I have done or what has happened to me? Jesus has not come through for me. Have I wasted my time and my energy? Is Jesus the one, or should I look for another?

IS JESUS THE ONE, OR SHOULD I LOOK FOR ANOTHER?

Jesus gives John's disciples this answer: "Go, report to John what you hear and see. Those who were blind are able to see. Those who were crippled are walking. People with skin diseases are cleansed. Those who were deaf now hear. Those who were dead are raised up. The poor have good news proclaimed to them. Happy are those who don't stumble and fall because of me" (verses 4-6).

John is Jesus' cousin and friend. Remember how he does the *in utero* leap when the pregnant Mary walks into the room to greet the pregnant Elizabeth (Luke 1:39-45)? Jesus tells John's disciples to look around them and report back to his friend. His miracles and his teachings are the answer. Go back, says Jesus, and tell my friend what he already knows. He has seen me heal people. He has seen me cure leprosy and liberate people from poverty. He knows that I am the King over all that would rob people of life. He has seen me conquer all of these things. Go back and remind John, my friend who is doubting and wavering, of what he has already seen and already knows. He knows, he has seen, that I am the King.

And then, like a good king, Jesus takes the focus off of himself and puts it back on his friend John. As John's disciples left, Jesus began teaching about who John was (verses 7-11). He told the crowds that John was a prophet, and even more than a prophet. John was the one spoken of by the prophet Malachi: "Look, I'm sending my messenger before you, who will prepare your way before you" (Matthew 11:10; Malachi 3:1). And then Jesus tells the crowds, "I assure you that no one who has ever been born is greater than John the Baptist. Yet whoever is least in the kingdom of heaven is greater than he" (Matthew 11:11). And all of this leads up to that head scratcher verse about the kingdom of heaven suffering violence or forcefully advancing.

Jesus is talking about his friend John, who announced the kingdom of heaven and is now suffering violence. But this same friend, who was once forceful and bold in his proclamation—bold enough to call Herod out on his sexual escapades—is now experiencing doubt about Jesus' identity as the King. Jesus has responded to John by reminding him of his miracles, of all the enemies that Jesus has conquered: blindness, disability, leprosy, deafness, poverty, even death. And yet, he has not fully conquered John. John still doubts, still wonders if he should wait for another. Jesus needs to conquer John, to drive out all of his doubt so that John can be sustained through his imprisonment with the knowledge that the true King is here.

When we keep the focus on John, we no longer need to decide between the two different readings of verse 12. These two possibilities come together, colliding in the person of John the Baptist and his wavering trust in Jesus. Is the kingdom of heaven violently attacked, or does the Kingdom forcefully advance? Yes! John suffers violence as a representative of the Kingdom. But John is also the one in whom the Kingdom needs to advance forcefully, conquering him so that all his doubts and hesitations are pushed out. Jesus and his followers are always under attack. And we are always called to forcefully, violently eliminate anything in our hearts that stands in his way. When we keep the focus on John, we see that both readings are true. Red State or Blue State? Yes. Ford or Chevy? Yes. Duke or Carolina? Yes.

The King and his Kingdom—and remember, the kingdom of heaven refers to life on earth under the reign of Jesus—has always been and will always be under assault. Even when Jesus was a baby, Herod wanted to kill him. He killed every baby in Bethlehem under two years old, and Jesus only survived because his family fled to Egypt (Matthew 2:1-18). When Jesus preached in his hometown of Nazareth, the people responded by trying to kill him (Luke 4:14-30). When the Romans and religious leaders thought Jesus got to be too much, they killed him on the cross. The King is always the victim of violence, always under attack.

In eastern China, the government has recently been on a campaign to demolish crosses and entire church buildings that they deem to be too eye-catching or too large. Fighting has led to injuries as church members try to protect their buildings and crosses. Large congregations have been forced to meet in alternative locations, and many feel they have been uprooted. The government claims that the crosses and church structures violate local building codes, but church members believe Christians are being targeted specifically.[2] The kingdom of heaven is always suffering violence in one way or another.

But here is the good news: The King and the Kingdom are always prevailing over those who attack them. As Jesus tells John, the King has already conquered blindness, disability, leprosy, and deafness. Jesus and his family escaped Herod; he won followers among his angry listeners; he rose from the dead. The church is growing where Christians are being persecuted. In those places where the kingdom of heaven is under assault, the kingdom of heaven is also forcefully advancing.

And the flip side? To follow Jesus with any real integrity means you do it forcefully, so that you ruthlessly, violently eliminate whatever holds you back from living in intimacy with him. Those others—King Herod, angry religious leaders, Roman authorities, hostile modern governments, even death—those are Jesus' enemies.

JESUS HAS TO CONQUER HIS FRIENDS BEFORE HE CONQUERS HIS ENEMIES.

But it's his friends that Jesus is more worried about! Jesus will always conquer his enemies, but he has yet to conquer his friends who do not follow him completely and faithfully. In the face of violence from Jesus' enemies, his friend John starts to waver, to question, to wonder if perhaps he should look to someone else.

Something tells me that in Matthew 11, Jesus was sending his lifelong friend John a message, urging him: "John, stop waffling! I liked you better when you were bold. I know you're down now and I know that can lead to doubts, but remember what you've seen and heard. You know who I am! You heard who I am! Stop waffling and start surrendering." With that in mind, here's my takeaway from this first head scratcher: *Jesus has to conquer his friends before he conquers his enemies*.

Jesus is the King, under continual assault, and he has conquered every enemy. So he insists on followers who have themselves been conquered. Some of you reading this consider yourselves to be Jesus' friends. You go to church. You attend study groups. You put some money in the offering plate. Some of you even sing that song "Friend of God" in your church. And some of you super-religious folks even raise your hands when you sing that song! But you know as well as I do that though you are his friend, you are not fully conquered. There are hidden or maybe not-so-hidden parts of you that you hold back. You hold out. Jesus wants us to be all-in citizens of the kingdom of heaven, while we content ourselves living as half-saved Christians.

You may have heard of the military leader from long ago who was receiving the surrender of an opposing general. As part of the surrender ceremony, the enemy general offered his hand in a handshake. The victorious general responded, "I cannot shake your hand, sir, until you first surrender your sword." What is your sword? What in your life stands in the way of your full surrender to Jesus? Is it your wallet? your temper? your eating disorder? your mistress? your mister? your marijuana? *Jesus has to conquer his friends before he conquers his enemies.*

You know what? I believe that a part of us—you and me and everyone else—bucks up against the love of God. We deeply need the love of God and we hate it at the same time. This is because we know that the love of God is not always gentle. It can sometimes be aggressive, even violent within our lives. We know that to be swamped by it means we will have to make some changes. And so we react against it, try to accept a little bit of it and resist the rest. And the result is a whole lot of half-saved Christians. I want you to stop hating God's love and allow yourself to be conquered by it. I want you to surrender your sword.

You know why I believe this is a vital message? We are all conquered by something. It could be a romantic interest or a toxic relationship. It could be ambition. Or money. In my family growing up, it was politics. It could be hobbies, TV shows, the Carolina Panthers, or Facebook. It could be laziness. Or pot. Or laziness brought on by pot. For me, it's my obsession with my reputation, my failure to recognize that if the kingdom were my priority, my reputation would take care of itself. We are all conquered by someone or something, and most of these things will rob us of life. Jesus wants us to be conquered by the prevailing Lord, the one whose intentions for us are good. Why not be conquered by the one whose desire is not to manipulate you but to elevate you? *Jesus has to conquer his friends before he conquers his enemies.*

WE ARE ALL CONQUERED BY SOMEONE OR SOMETHING.

Letting Jesus conquer us means that we ruthlessly, forcefully replace all that not-good stuff with things that are better. We couple our passion with his power. Instead of laziness, how about great reading? When it comes to money, instead of hoarding, keeping, scheming, why not invest in God's kingdom? Even invest with your time. As much as I hate to admit it, we have a lot of what I call cul-de-sac Christians in today's church. Even at the church I serve, Good Shepherd United Methodist Church. Where does a cul-de-sac go? This is not a trick question: It goes nowhere! We have a lot of Christians going nowhere—people who want to be fed, inspired, entertained, but don't give anything back. People who drop off their kids but refuse to serve and get involved themselves. Why not invest your time and energy in the kingdom of heaven?

There's a reason the church (in general) has not always been successful with the next generation. A lot of our children grow up overchurched and underwhelmed—underwhelmed by half-saved Christians. Passing the faith on to the next generation doesn't just happen. It takes parents speaking truth intentionally and consistently at home. And it takes at least one other voice speaking the truth outside of home. It takes one or two consistent, integrity-filled voices from the community echoing what mom and dad are saying at home. That is why Jill Stuckey and Toby Hoving may be two names you've never heard of before, but they are two of the most important names in my family. Because Jill was that extra voice in my daughter's life

and Toby the extra voice in my son's. But get this: You don't shape
and mold the preacher's kids by being a half-saved Christian. They
signed up! They served! Jill and Toby had been conquered. And
because they had been conquered, they were able to pour themselves
into the cause of the conquering King. Let's exercise some violence to
the half-saved Christian living inside each of us who call on Christ.
Jesus has to conquer his friends before he conquers his enemies.

I'm glad in retrospect that I scratched my head over Matthew
11:12 and didn't throw this whole series out the window. I'm glad
this isn't the first chapter of *Easy to Understand Bible Verses*. By
digging into Matthew 11, I was able to see that the Kingdom and
the King will always be subjected to attack, and that the King will
conquer all of his attackers. But I also discovered that the ones he
really needs to conquer are his friends. I'm able to see that he has
me in his sights as target number one. And I suppose he has you in
his sights as well.

Questions for Reflection and Discussion

Write responses and other thoughts in the space below each
question. If you are discussing the book in a small group, prepare
for the meeting by writing answers in advance.

1. Name some verses, teachings, or longer passages in
    Scripture that have truly caused you to scratch you head.
    How do you make sense of them?

2. What is your typical response when you encounter a verse in Scripture that you don't understand? What do you do to try to understand it better? How can "Context Is Everything" help you with some of these verses?

3. How did John the Baptist respond to the violence that he suffered?

4. What answer does Jesus give to John's question, and what does Jesus mean by it? Do you think John would have been satisfied with Jesus' answer?

THE VIOLENT BEAR IT AWAY

5. Matthew 11:12 suggests that Jesus and his followers will suffer violence. Where do you see this prediction coming true in our world?

6. Describe a time when you felt like your Christian faith was under assault. How did you react?

7. Matthew 11:12 also suggests that we must allow Christ and the kingdom of heaven to conquer us. To what extent are you conquered by Christ?

8. Where have you seen evidence that Jesus is the conquering King in our world or in your own life?

9. We are all conquered by something. What has conquered you? What is the sword that you have to surrender?

Become a Conquered Person

Name one thing you'll do differently this week to forcefully advance the cause of your own faith. As you pray the prayer below, "Come out with your hands up." Lift your hands to God in surrender, signifying that you will allow Jesus to conquer you completely in this area of your life.

Closing Prayer

Lord, you are a conquering King and you want to liberate us from self-destruction. Thank you for your abundant love, which is the key to abundant, eternal life. We come to you with our hands up, surrendering to you because you are Lord. Glory to you in the highest. Amen.

Daily Scripture Readings

This week, read the following Scripture passages. As you read, pay attention to how Christ is seeking to advance the Kingdom in your own heart and life.

Monday: Matthew 11:1-15
Tuesday: Luke 7:18-35
Wednesday: Matthew 13:1-43
Thursday: Matthew 13:44-58
Friday: Mark 4:1-34

1. From "Gunmen Kill Medical Aid Workers in Afghanistan," by Rod Nordland in *The New York Times*, August 2010. *www.nytimes.com/2010/08/08/world/asia/08afghan.html?pagewanted=all&_r=0*. Accessed 27 March 2015.

2. From "China's Christians Fear New Persecution after Latest Wave of Church Demolitions," by Brice Pedroletti in *The Guardian*, July 4, 2014. *www.theguardian.com/world/2014/jul/05/china-christianity-wenzhou-zhejiang-churches*. Accessed 27 March 2015.

2

HATE YOUR
FATHER AND MOTHER

Whoever comes to me and doesn't hate father and mother, spouse and children, and brothers and sisters—yes, even one's own life— cannot be my disciple. (Luke 14:26)

Note: This sermon was delivered on Father's Day, 2014, at Good Shepherd United Methodist Church.

Well, happy Father's Day to you too, Jesus! Can you imagine all the grumbling and fussing and *head scratching* that must have followed when Jesus said those words? No doubt entire families had come out to hear him preach and to see him perform miracles. Apparently he didn't care too much about ensuring those same crowds would come back next Sunday, did he? I suppose there was a young woman in the crowd, all excited about Jesus, who had brought her father along with her. She had to work and cajole and beg her father even to come because he usually spent Sundays sleeping off the previous night's festivities. And—great day!—she finally got him to come and they'd just settled into their seats when BAM, Jesus dropped the line: *hate your father*. And the young woman just wanted to crawl into a hole and die because of the way this supposed Savior embarrassed her.

There was probably a young man in the crowd too, who had finally brought his mother to meet Jesus. Mom was a faithful Jew, very comfortable in her religion and its rituals, and she didn't like much of what she had heard about Jesus. He seemed way too . . . contemporary. Too permissive. But to appease her eager son, she came to the gathering to hear Jesus. And just when she was starting to feel better, thinking maybe there was something to this guy after all, Jesus blasted her very reason for being: hate your mother. And she didn't wait for her son to climb into a hole and die; she just picked up her purse and marched out. Right down the center aisle!

I think many moms and dads and grandmoms and granddads feel the same way about these words in the twenty-first century. They're just so objectionable. Harmful. Yes, even hateful. It takes us by surprise even to hear Jesus talking about hate in the first place. We have always thought Jesus was about love, not hate. Our beloved Bible verse is John 3:16, "God so loved the world. . . . " But then we open up the Bible to Luke 14:26 and see Jesus encouraging hatred, as if there aren't enough spewers of hate out there already. So how in the world do with deal with this particular head scratcher?

The answer is, very carefully. To see what Jesus is doing here, we have to pull back from our laser focus on the one verse that seems so confusing to see what's going on in the whole scene. Just as critically, it helps to know how Jesus and his contemporaries used language. It is important for us to recognize that Jesus often used exaggeration to make a point. It was a rhetorical device, much like speaking in parables or using rhetorical questions. On more than one occasion, Jesus and other ancient teachers used over-the-top, unbelievable, exaggerated language not because they meant it literally, but because it drew an unforgettable picture in the minds of their listeners.

Take, for example, Matthew 5:30, where Jesus says, "If your right hand causes you to fall into sin, chop it off and throw it away.

It's better that you lose a part of your body than that your whole body go into hell." We take Scripture pretty seriously at the church I serve, but nobody takes Jesus that literally! Another example occurs just before this, in Matthew 5:28-29: "I say to you that every man who looks at a woman lustfully has already committed adultery in his heart. And if your right eye causes you to fall into sin, tear it out and throw it away. It's better that you lose a part of your body than that your whole body be thrown into hell."

Now, if we didn't think Jesus was exaggerating, using over-the-top language to make a point in these verses, every man in Good Shepherd—and every other church—would be blind.

CONTEXT IS EVERYTHING.

We know (thankfully) that Jesus is not telling us literally to cut off our own hands or gouge out our own eyes in Matthew 5:28-30.

The same is true for Luke 14:26. Jesus is not teaching his hearers literally to hate their fathers and mothers, spouses and children, brothers and sisters. What strikes me, though, is that taking Jesus literally here might actually be easier for a lot of us. Think about that for a minute. Some of us, if only for a short while, already hate our parents or our brothers and sisters. We don't need any help from Jesus to get there. Some people have suffered the deepest kinds of betrayal at the hands of those who should have loved them the most. Oh, their parents might have been model moms and dads in public, but shocking things happened when they got behind closed doors. Some have suffered physical, psychological, or sexual abuse at the hands of their family members. These know, sadly, all about hating those whom you are "supposed" to love. For others, perhaps it was not so traumatic, but nonetheless infuriating. Approval that was conditional based on their performance. A constant flow of criticism about their appearance. Favoritism that led to the unhealthiest of sibling rivalries. Truly, taking Jesus literally in Luke 14:26 doesn't require any kind of supernatural effort for many of us; it comes as naturally as breathing.

Except the fact remains that Jesus is exaggerating here, painting a vivid picture to make an enduring point. And the point he makes is truthfully more challenging and more comprehensive than if we were to take it all literally.

To understand this point fully, it is helpful to see where the whole scene starts. In the last chapter, I told you about C.I.E., Context Is Everything. To figure out a head scratcher verse—or really any passage in the Bible—we need to see what comes before it and what comes after it, understanding it within the fabric of the whole story where it occurs.

Here is the scene in which we find Luke 14:26:

> [25] Large crowds were traveling with Jesus. Turning to them, he said, [26] "Whoever comes to me and doesn't hate father and mother, spouse and children, and brothers and sisters—yes, even one's own life—cannot be my disciple. [27] Whoever doesn't carry their own cross and follow me cannot be my disciple.
>
> [28] "If one of you wanted to build a tower, wouldn't you first sit down and calculate the cost, to determine whether you have enough money to complete it? [29] Otherwise, when you have laid the foundation but couldn't finish the tower, all who see it will begin to belittle you. [30] They will say, 'Here's the person who began construction and couldn't complete it!' [31] Or what king would go to war against another king without first sitting down to consider whether his ten thousand soldiers could go up against the twenty thousand coming against him? [32] And if he didn't think he could win, he would send a representative to discuss terms of peace while his enemy was still a long way off. [33] In the same way, none of you who are unwilling to give up all of your possessions can be my disciple.

We see in the first verse that Jesus was being followed by "large crowds." He was becoming a spectacle. Jesus had been telling great parables—the good Samaritan (Luke 10:25-37) and the rich fool (Luke 12:16-21), for example—and he would soon tell one of his greatest, the prodigal son (Luke 15:11-32). He had healed (Luke 5:12-26). He had performed miracles (Luke 7:11-17; 9:10-17). He had challenged authority (Luke 11:37-52). Obviously, something about his message, and about him as a messenger, connected with people. Jesus generated a buzz, and "large crowds" traveled with him. And of course, if any of Luke 14:25 ever described me, my question would be, "How do I get them to come back? How do I make sure I have the right combination of accepting and challenging people so that they can't wait to come back next Sunday?" That is the goal for most modern preachers: Attract a crowd and keep it.

IT'S TIME TO SEPARATE THE SERIOUS FROM THE SUPERFICIAL.

Evidently, it is not a goal that Jesus shared. I cannot help but think Luke puts this little detail in this particular place on purpose. Jesus knew he was in danger of becoming a spectacle, a sideshow attraction, and so what follows was designed to separate serious disciples from those who were only casually interested. Jesus wanted to distinguish between those looking to enjoy a show and those wanting to love a Savior. So to accomplish his goal, Jesus dove into those intimate and powerful relationships with an absurd call to hate those we love. He then followed that up with two stories about things that are halfway done: a story of a half-built building (14:28-30) and a half-fought war (14:31-32).

The Heritage Tower. Photograph by Matt Crace

If we put all this together, we get the following picture: Jesus is gathering a crowd, and he decides it's time to separate the serious from the superficial. He says the head-scratching statement about hating father and mother, spouse and children, brothers and sisters, and then he tells a story of a half-built building and a half-fought war. When it's all laid out it becomes pretty clear what Jesus is doing. He is launching a preemptive strike, so to speak, against people who halfway follow him. Against people who partially accept him. Jesus says these words in this way because he knows there is a great danger of following someone as magnetic as he is: People will partially accept him and casually attach themselves to him. Is there anything worse than something that is halfway done?

Within shouting distance of Good Shepherd Church stands a half-built tower. Some of you may remember the PTL (short for Praise The Lord) Ministry of Jim and Tammy Faye Bakker that had its heyday in the mid-1980's. Well, the Heritage Tower, a combination hotel and condominium complex, was designed to be the crown jewel of the entire PTL campus near Fort Mill, South Carolina. It had just "topped out" in construction in early 1987 when the scandal that brought down the Bakkers and their ministry erupted. Since that time, the tower has stood uncompleted. Twenty-one stories tall, but no infrastructure within. As you might suspect, the ensuing twenty-eight years have not been kind to the building: The masonry is crumbling, the stairwells are collapsing, and the entire site is ringed with signage warning would-be trespassers of the dangers within.

Many of the people of Good Shepherd Church live with this eyesore literally in their backyards. There is even a Facebook page dedicated to its demolition: *www.facebook.com/pages/Tear-Down-the-Morningstar-Tower/209143829117670*

This tower is an ugly blight in the middle of an otherwise lovely community. But more to the point, it is an enduring testimony to the destructive power of things that are half-done, of jobs left incomplete.

That's the way it is with things that are partially done, isn't it? Imagine how aspiring collegians would feel if they opened letters from the universities to which they applied, with the message: "Congratulations, we sort of accept you!" Or what if someone partially accepted a marriage proposal? A man nervously asks one of the most important questions of his life, "Will you marry me?" To which he hears the reply, "Maybe. Sort of, almost. Partially." "Mom, dad, I'd like you to meet my sort-of fiancée!" A partial acceptance has all the satisfaction of a half-eaten meal or a half-mowed lawn. It's like getting half of a haircut or building half of a house. Jesus knows that the greatest danger to his kingdom is having a collection of partial followers. People who begin to build towers—and lives—only to abandon them when things become too challenging or too painful.

Might there be some people reading this book who only partially follow Jesus? I know when that was true for me. I was young, newly out of college and newly married, and caught up in trying to make my way in a secular career. During that time, I had a lot of priorities, and it became very easy for me to just edge faith out of my life. I allowed God to have the hour from eleven to twelve on Sunday morning, but kept the rest of the time for myself. You know what I noticed during that season of my life? I had a shocking amount of relational conflict with people. There was so much conflict with coworkers, family, in-laws, even people I played tennis with. At the time I just figured I was hanging around a lot of people who were hard to get along with. In retrospect, it dawned on me that I was the common denominator in all those relationships. It wasn't that other people had problems; it was that my relationship with Jesus Christ wasn't living. My relationship with Christ was flatlining, and chaos in my other relationships was the result. I was only partially accepting Jesus' ownership of my life.

Does some of this sound familiar? Do you fit Jesus in when he is convenient or when you really need him, but edge him out when he is inconvenient? Perhaps you read and listen to the Bible, but do so selectively, only paying attention to your favorite parts. Maybe you started reading in Genesis, found it confusing when you arrived at Exodus, and became thoroughly bored by the time you got to Leviticus. So you stopped reading and refused to commit your whole mind to following Jesus. Perhaps you had questions about faith and science, but instead of addressing them seriously you chose to just give up on faith because it was easier that way. Or perhaps you want to commit to Jesus but want to reserve some small part of yourself. You have some dark things in your closet that nobody knows about but you and God, and sometimes you're not sure even if God knows about them. And every once in a while you need to go and nurse those things, because they are more important to you than you want to admit.

You know what is the most common phrase I hear from people who halfway follow Jesus? *I wish.* They look back on earlier points in their lives and say, "I wish . . ." I wish I had gone on that mission trip. I wish I had taken that class. I wish I hadn't fallen for that guy. I wish I hadn't spent that money so foolishly. I wish I could stop my self-destruction. What really happens is, people who halfway follow and partially accept settle for far less than the full life God wants for them. Jesus claims everything, owns everything, calls us to give everything. And we try to get by with less, settle for a smaller portion. We try to get by with giving less of ourselves to him, and we receive less of out of life in return. And what are the consequences of partial acceptance? Look at the last part of Luke 14:26: "cannot be my disciple."

Chilling words, to be sure. "Cannot be my disciple." This is a far cry from "Jesus meek and mild," a far different picture from "Jesus loves the little children." This is Jesus unfiltered. This is Jesus devoid of so much of the sentimentality with which we enshroud him.

And these ominous words lead to this unmistakable bottom line, whether we hear them on Father's Day or any other day: *Partial acceptance is complete rejection.*

That's right. There is no difference between the two. Halfway following is not following at all. If you have settled, you have denied. If you have dabbled, you have forsaken. If you want to have Jesus as your Savior but not as your Lord, you will have him as neither. If you want to do and be the barest minimum you can and still become a part of God's kingdom, you won't make it. That's when the head scratching becomes heartbreaking. That's why Jesus

PARTIAL ACCEPTANCE IS COMPLETE REJECTION.

used such over-the-top, shocking language in verse 26, saying, "Whoever does not hate father and mother, spouse and children, and brothers and sisters—yes, even one's own life—cannot be my disciple." The consequences of not understanding him are huge and eternal. There is no such thing as safe, convenient discipleship. *Partial acceptance is complete rejection.*

Jesus' message is about loyalty. Remember, he used over-the-top language and did not literally mean for us to "hate" father and mother. However, Jesus wants nothing less than our highest loyalty. If there is ever a competition between following Jesus and pleasing even our own families, Jesus wins.

Sometimes, following Jesus as your highest loyalty is not as difficult as you think it will be. In my own life, nobody—and I mean nobody—in my family expected or wanted me to be a pastor. If you had asked them what they expected for me, they may have said government work, law, or education. Preacher? No, not a one on either side of the family tree in forever. For many of my kin, orthodox Christian faith is almost incomprehensible. So when I sensed that God was calling me into ministry, that conversation where I told them was awkward and gut wrenching. And yet the glorious news is that now, as the years have gone by and they see that I love this life, they have come to love the church I serve. Many in my family keep up with Good Shepherd, and they are proud of what we stand for and accomplish in serving God. So now it's great news for my family that Talbot is a pastor. And as a side benefit, they have somebody to do their funeral when they die. Now that's a perk of having clergy in the family that you don't hear about very much! So when my loyalties came into conflict, I chose to follow Christ fully even over my family—in a sense "hating" them—but it turned out great in the end.

THERE IS NO SUCH THING AS SAFE, CONVENIENT DISCIPLESHIP.

Unfortunately, I cannot say the same for everyone. At Good Shepherd Church, we partner with pastors in the Kandhamal region of the state of Odisha, on the east coast of India. Whenever these pastors perform a baptism, the stakes are high. Each person who is baptized goes under the water a Hindu and comes up out of the water a Christian. And they do so at the risk that they will be cut off from family, from village, and from professional possibility for the rest of their lives. These folks stop worshiping local gods and goddesses and start worshiping the one true God, and to mark that transformation they go public by getting wet. For a few of them it might be the kiss of death. And we in America complain when people say, "Happy Holidays" instead of "Merry Christmas!" Really?! People are dying because they love Jesus and "hate" family, and we call in the Christian cavalry because of what someone says to us at Target in December?! Good God. You know what these faithful, courageous believers discover in India when they risk losing family for the sake of gaining Jesus? The blood applied to their sin is more important than the blood flowing under their skin. They may be related to mom and dad and siblings by blood, but that blood is nothing compared to what was shed on the cross for them. And when they come up out of that water, they are more related to you and me and other Christians than they are to their own biological families. That's the new creation. That's the church, and we get to be part of it.

THE BLOOD APPLIED TO YOUR SIN IS MORE IMPORTANT THAN THE BLOOD FLOWING UNDER YOUR SKIN.

Speaking of geography, I recently learned something from Devin Tharp, our Student and Family Ministries Pastor at Good Shepherd. He moved to Charlotte from Wisconsin, and what he shared with me snapped into focus when I realized that I had been through something similar. Where Devin had previously worked in student ministry, there was not a strong church culture. So if a student decided to become part of their youth group, it usually came with a cost. There was no parental pressure to join youth group, no social expectation for students to go, and at school it could hurt rather than help a student's reputation. And so because there was a real cost, there was a great commitment. If you wanted to be in student ministry where Devin served, you had to be all in. In the Carolinas, where I serve, we're in the Bible Belt where there is some kind of cultural expectation to be part of a church. It is so much easier to be casual about church and youth group involvement. Because there's little cost, there can be lower commitment.

Devin's thoughts made complete sense to me because I had lived the same experience. As I indicated earlier, I grew up in a family that had largely fallen out of church, so when I came to faith as a seventeen-year-old, there was no point in partially accepting anything. My conversion to faith *was* my teenage rebellion! My popularity at home did not increase when I decided to follow Jesus. Then when I was a little older, the atmosphere at my college in New Jersey was strongly anti-Christian, even in the eighties. But there was a small group of us who were Christians on that campus. And because there were so few of us, we banded together and became stronger, not weaker. In both of those environments, at home and in college, I really grew as a Christian.

So do I teach parents to stop raising their kids in church so they'll rebel into faith as teenagers? Do I think we should all move to non-Christian communities, perhaps all the way to India? No, of course not. But in Charlotte, where I live, there is a parkway named after the evangelist Billy Graham. In such a place, it can be acceptable to be connected to a church. There are enough cultural assumptions here that you can get away with partially following Jesus. In our culture, partially following Jesus is acceptable to everybody. Everybody except Jesus, who says to those of us who accept him halfway, "You cannot be my disciple." Head scratching turns to heartbreaking. *Partial acceptance is complete rejection.*

I don't want you to settle. Partial acceptance results in a lot of things that are less than the life God has in mind for us. Relational trauma and chaos come from partial acceptance. Compulsive, repetitive self-destruction comes from partial acceptance. A despairing view of life, wondering "what's the point?" comes from partial acceptance. Anxiety about the next life comes from partial acceptance. On the other hand, every person I know who started "hating" even their life, their old life, for the sake of fully following Jesus has an overwhelming serenity. There is a peacefulness, a deep sense that their lives belong to God and their future is in God's hands.

A while back at Good Shepherd, I did a sermon series called Wash Me! And during that series, we e-mailed daily prayers to the congregation. Each day during the series, a different prayer would be emailed at 9:00 A.M. to supplement the weekly message. One person at Good Shepherd, who is relatively new to a living relationship with Jesus, also happens to be a particularly good e-mail communicator with me. Now, if you are good e-mail communicator with me, chances are I will give you something to do on behalf of the church. And so during this series, I asked her to write one of the daily prayers, even though she has only known Christ in a living relationship for a short time. She was hesitant at first, but she eventually agreed to do it and it went great. We e-mailed her prayer, and it went out to over three thousand people. I'm sure she was nervous to have her prayer read by so many people. But here is how she described it afterwards:

I love this! And I love how much I have changed for the better this past year.

Those words don't come from any partial accepter, but from someone who fully follows Jesus. I want her story to be yours.

Questions for Reflection and Discussion

Write responses and other thoughts in the space below each question. If you are discussing the book in a small group, prepare for the meeting by writing answers in advance.

1. Recall (or research) some times when Jesus used exaggeration to make his point. Why do you think he used this method of communication in those situations?

2. Think back to a time when you did something "halfway" (a school or work project, hobby, specific responsibility, and so forth). What was that experience like, and what was the result?

3. Is there anything that you have started but left unfinished, like the half-built tower? Why did you start, and what prevented you from completing it?

4. What does it mean to only "partially accept" Jesus? What does a life of partial acceptance look like in our culture in the early twenty-first century?

5. Think of a time in your life when you feel that you only followed Jesus halfway. What do you wish you had done differently in those circumstances?

6. When, if ever, has following Christ cost you something? How "expensive" was that cost? Did the cost ever cause you to consider abandoning your faith or the church?

7. When has your church or community made a costly commitment to follow Christ? What was the result of this commitment? What other priorities had to be sacrificed in order to do this?

8. What are the most important loyalties in your life right now?

9. In what way is God calling you to "hate" these things in order to be a true disciple of Christ?

10. Name an area of your present life in which you have only partially accepted Christ. What would it mean for you to follow Jesus completely in this respect?

Reject Partial Acceptance

On the following page you will find a declaration, a statement that you will reject an easy, convenient discipleship in order to follow Jesus with your complete loyalty. In the space provided, write the most important areas of your life in which you are only partially following Jesus. Take several minutes and meditate on the cost of fully accepting Christ, recognizing the changes you'll have to make in behavior or attitude. If the Spirit leads you, sign your name to the page, signifying your commitment to follow Jesus completely. If you have a smartphone or other mobile device with a camera, take a photo of your signature and set it as your phone's background or wallpaper for the next week (or longer). Whenever you see it, remember that you have rejected partial acceptance to be a true disciple of Jesus.

If you wish, you may share the photo with others via Twitter, Facebook, Instagram, or another social media site using the hashtag #HeadScratchers. If you are reading the book in a group setting, consider printing a single copy of the document and having all group members sign it. Then you can display it in your meeting room through the rest of the study.

Closing Prayer

Lord, we take these moments to confess the ways that we have only partially accepted you. We now know that is really full rejection. Protect us from our own worst enemies—complacency, selfishness, and arrogance. As a community, we surrender ourselves from the tops of our heads to the bottoms of our feet. Amen.

Daily Scripture Readings

Monday: Matthew 5:1-20
Tuesday: Matthew 5:21-48
Wednesday: Matthew 10:1-25
Thursday: Matthew 10:26-42
Friday: Psalm 23:1-6

A Declaration of Full Discipleship

I confess Jesus Christ as my Savior and put my trust in him. I accept the freedom and power God gives me to turn away from sin and embrace a life of discipleship. I am called to follow Jesus completely, not partially. This is the way to full, abundant life. Despite this calling, I have partially accepted Jesus, seeking only to follow him halfway. Below I list the areas of my life where other things have stood in the way. In the following ways, I confess that I have stopped short of fully following Jesus:

_____

_____

_____

_____

_____

_____

_____

_____

_____

If I completely follow Christ, I know that it will be costly in every aspect of my life, including those listed above. It will change my priorities; it will change my attitudes; it will change how I live. I have counted the cost, and with God's help I commit to living as a full disciple of Jesus Christ.

Signed: _____

Date: _____

3

THE GATES OF HADES

I tell you that you are Peter. And I'll build my church on this rock. The gates of the underworld won't be able to stand against it. (Matthew 16:18)

What is the first rule of real estate? Location, location, location. Where you buy a house or build an office park is more important than the kind of house or park that you get. It's all about where a particular structure is located. That's why a bungalow in the Myers Park area of Charlotte costs around a million dollars. The same house down in the Steele Creek community, where Good Shepherd is located, costs . . . well, a good deal less. No million-dollar bungalows in my neighborhood! Location, location, location.

I mention that first rule of real estate because nowhere is it more true in Scripture than with this head scratcher, Matthew 16:18. Jesus says to one of his disciples, "I tell you that you are Peter, and on this rock I will build my church, and the gates of Hades will not overcome it" (New International Version). Now, trying to figure out what the "gates of Hades" (or "gates of the underworld") are is a real head scratcher. But it turns out that *where* Jesus said this is just

51

as important as *what* he said. Remember, we have been discovering together how *Context Is Everything*, and in this case the context is not merely literary; it's geographical. The first rule of real estate—location, location, location—can help us understand what this head scratcher is all about. So where is Jesus when he utters these words?

Here's the whole story in Matthew 16:13-20:

> ¹³ Now when Jesus came to the area of Caesarea Philippi, he asked his disciples, "Who do people say the Human One is?"
> ¹⁴ They replied, "Some say John the Baptist, others Elijah, and still others Jeremiah or one of the other prophets."
> ¹⁵ He said, "And what about you? Who do you say that I am?"
> ¹⁶ Simon Peter said, "You are the Christ, the Son of the living God."
> ¹⁷ Then Jesus replied, "Happy are you, Simon son of Jonah, because no human has shown this to you. Rather my Father who is in heaven has shown you. ¹⁸ I tell you that you are Peter. And I'll build my church on this rock. The gates of the underworld won't be able to stand against it. ¹⁹ I'll give you the keys of the kingdom of heaven. Anything you fasten on earth will be fastened in heaven. Anything you loosen on earth will be loosened in heaven." ²⁰ Then he ordered the disciples not to tell anybody that he was the Christ.

Verse 13 tells us where Jesus was when he spoke with his disciples: Caesarea Philippi. That is Jesus' location, location, location when he utters this head scratcher. So what's the big deal with that place? What does it have to do with the story? *Only everything.* Caesarea Philippi was located about twenty-five miles north of the Sea of Galilee, close to where Jesus spent most of his time teaching, healing, and working miracles. It stood at the base of a mountain called Mount Hermon. And Caesarea Philippi was, for lack of a better term, a hot zone for idol worship. Even before it was a Roman city, that place had been a religious site dedicated to the worship of other gods for hundreds of years, going back far earlier than the time of Jesus.

Long before the first century A.D., the area was not yet called Caesarea Philippi. Its original inhabitants were some of the Canaanite people, Israel's neighbors who are mentioned throughout the Old Testament. And the Canaanites worshiped a god called Baal, who was a well-known storm god at that time. If you read the Old Testament, especially First and Second Kings, you will find that the Israelites were often tempted to worship Baal. This was, of course, a clear violation of the first of the Ten Commandments, where God commands Israel, "You must have no other gods before me" (Exodus 20:3). But frequently the people of Israel wanted to hedge their bets and cover their bases, in the event that the Lord didn't come through for them. They would worship the Lord, but then go ahead and worship Baal too. They kept Baal in their hip pocket—you know, just in case.

LOCATION, LOCATION, LOCATION

The Canaanites, meanwhile, had long believed that Baal was the god of storms, and so in their minds he was responsible for the seasonal cycles of rain, new life, and fertility. The Israelites were tempted to worship this Canaanite god almost from the moment of their first interactions with their new neighbors. The area that became Caesarea Philippi was an important site of Baal worship. Twice in the Old Testament, the area around Mount Hermon is called Baal-Hermon, showing how closely that god was identified with that region (Judges 3:3; 1 Chronicles 5:23). What should have been *terra non-grata* for faithful Israelites instead became a temptation too enticing to resist.

Much later, this territory came under control of the Greeks, who worshiped the god Pan, among others. Traditionally, Pan was worshiped at natural sites, such as caves or springs, rather than temples. Now here's another significant fact about the site that became Caesarea Philippi: It was located at the base of sheer, rocky walls containing caves and a natural spring. With the arrival of the Greeks, this spring became an important site for the worship of Pan; the Greeks even called the spring Paneas in honor of their god's name. Pan had much in common with Baal, beyond the fact that both were worshiped in this region. Pan was not a storm deity, but like Baal, Pan was associated with fertility and the renewal of spring in his own way.

Pan's association with fertility contained an added dimension: He was also a god of sexuality. Much of the mythology surrounding Pan recounted his sexual exploits. And the worship of Pan at the mouth of these caves at Caesarea Philippi involved . . . how do I say this delicately? Human acts of fertility and sexuality. Promiscuity. Going to the "church of Pan," so to speak, meant that you drank all the alcohol you could while sleeping with as many partners as possible. All to honor their god! I don't care how good your praise band or teaching programs are, it is hard for any church to compete against that sort of thing for the men's attention! And all this worship of Baal and Pan—the Rain Maker and the Sex God—had occurred in and around Caesarea Philippi. The city was not only a hot zone for idols, but it was also a bit of a red-light district for people in the area.

Now fast forward to Jesus' own day. After the Greeks came the Romans, who conquered the region and established their own government. The Romans ruled during the time of Jesus—Herod, Pilate, and the other names you've heard, after all, were proxy rulers for Rome stationed in Judea and Galilee. And one of these proxy Roman rulers gave our city its name: Herod Philip wanted to honor the emperor, Caesar Augustus, so he named the city Caesarea. Later it came to be known as Caesarea Philippi, after Philip, because other Roman cities were also named Caesarea. It turns out that kissing up to the emperor was a popular thing to do!

The Roman rulers claimed supreme authority and even divinity, so that they should be worshiped as gods. Calling the city Caesarea was appropriate for Herod Philip. It was a way to acknowledge the Roman identity of the city and its inhabitants, as well as the lordship of Caesar who ruled all of Rome's territory. This was the kind of city where you had an ongoing loyalty oath: Caesar is Lord. Caesar's power loomed large at Caesarea Philippi. It might have felt like the District of Columbia, with its constant reminders of who controlled the government.

All of a sudden, it matters quite a bit that Jesus was here, in Caesarea Philippi, when he spoke to Peter and his other disciples. Against this backdrop of idol worship, promiscuity, and Caesar's power, Jesus stands up and presses his followers about his own identity. It's as if he invites them to comparison shop and see that there is no comparison at all. Through where he is—location, location, location—this mere Jewish carpenter deliberately sets himself up against all the religions and powers of the world. He asks his disciples, "Who do people say the Human One is?" (verse 13). They give the usual answers they've been hearing: John the Baptist, Elijah, Jeremiah, or one of the prophets. But Jesus pushes the issue, wanting them to answer for themselves: "Who do you say that I am?" (verse 15).

And that's when Simon Peter makes his bold declaration: "You are the Christ, the Son of the living God" (verse 16). In the shadow of a rock face wall, the one whose name means "rock" steps up, saying that Jesus is the Messiah they've all been waiting for. In the very place where other gods have been worshiped—false gods, lifeless gods, dead gods—Peter says that Jesus is the Son of the living God. In a place named after Caesar, Peter declares that Jesus, not Rome's ruler, is Lord. Peter makes this declaration for the first time here, at Caesarea Philippi, surrounded by the false teachings of sexual immorality, rain-making gods, and Caesar's absolute power. It is at this place, in a moment of courage and clarity, that Peter declares truth in the midst of lies: Jesus is the Son of the living God. Jesus is the Christ, the Messiah. Jesus is Lord and there is no other. Location, location, location indeed.

Jesus affirms Peter's response, telling him that his insight is a revelation from God. "Happy are you, Simon son of Jonah, because no human has shown this to you. Rather my Father who is in heaven has shown you. I tell you that you are Peter. And I'll build my church on this rock" (verses 17-18). Peter's name means "rock," and Jesus promises that he will build his church upon the person and profession of Peter. And then comes the head scratcher: "The gates of the underworld won't be able to stand against it" (verse 18). A more literal translation is "the gates of Hades will not overcome it" (NIV). Hades. The underworld. Huh? Why does Jesus start talking about Hades right after Peter's bold confession of faith and Jesus' equally bold promise about Peter's foundational role for the church?

HADES IS A HOLDING PATTERN.

Again, remember the location. They were at Caesarea Philippi, with its caves and natural spring close by. It was a place that lent itself to association with the underworld. Today, we often think of Hades as another word for hell. We might use them interchangeably, or maybe we use Hades when we want to be polite and avoid offensive language. But in ancient thought, Hades had a different meaning. The Jews and Greeks of Jesus' time and earlier did not have similar ideas of heaven and hell to what we have today. Instead, they thought of Hades, the underworld, as a place where everyone went when they died. It was a murky, fuzzy, shadowy sort of sub-existence, full of lifeless, bodiless spirits. If you think that sounds depressing, you are right! In the Greek epic *The Odyssey*, the hero Odysseus travels to Hades and speaks with the dead warrior Achilles. Achilles tells him that he would rather be a slave on earth than the ruler over all the lifeless dead in Hades.[1] The underworld was full of confusion and uncertainty, something far less than actual life. It was, in many ways, a holding pattern. Like when you're in a jet and it circles the airport for endless minutes waiting for an opportunity to land. You could compare it to being in line at the DMV waiting for hours to get your driver's license. Or perhaps it's like you're in traffic at that one intersection in town where the cars stretch forever at 5:30 on a Friday evening. In Charlotte, it's Gold Hill Road and Highway 160, but every city has its own. As the ancients thought of it, Hades is a place of hesitation, anxiety, apathy, uncertainty, and frustration. Hades is a holding pattern.

So much for Hades, but what about gates? Jesus tells Peter that "the gates of Hades" won't be able to overcome the church. Are the gates of Hades—whatever those are—attacking the church in some sort of odd visual Jesus wants to portray?

To understand what he means, it's good to remember that gates can keep people in as well as they keep people out. Cities and fortresses have gates, but so do prisons (see, for instance, Acts 12:10). Gates hold in, restrain, and limit. Jesus isn't talking about hell attacking the church here; he's talking about Hades keeping people locked up. In one sense, Jesus is saying that even death itself is no match for the church. As the Son of the living God, Jesus will restore life even to those who have died! But Jesus' words can also be understood in another sense. Think about what Hades symbolizes, if it's that shadowy, murky place of the dead. It is a holding pattern, symbolizing apathy and indecision. Hades is just going through the motions, marking the time with no purpose or life. That's what the "gates of Hades" do. They limit people, imprison people, by keeping them locked up in apathy and indecision. These gates keep people in a permanent holding pattern, going nowhere forever. Hades is not attacking us; it's trying to limit us.

Could it be that Jesus used these words—this head scratcher—because he knew that apathy and indecision are the very things that would threaten to hold back the church and its people? Think of all the ways that churches and the people in them can become jaded and frustrated, to the point where they just mark time without ever going anywhere. The spirit of apathy is one of the biggest obstacles that the

TRUTH LIBERATES WHAT APATHY LIMITS.

church faces. A preacher friend once told me that he had decided to stop taking risks in ministry because all the people in the church wanted him to do was carry, marry, and bury: carry babies to baptism, marry couples, and bury the dead during funerals. So he had stopped trying to do more than that. The people saw church as a series of rituals they observed, life stages they celebrated, and functions they took part in. There was no call, no desire for a living relationship with Jesus. I look back in my own rear view mirror, and I can identify seasons where I led Good Shepherd straight into a similar murkiness. You may have heard the old saying, "if there's a mist in the pulpit there will be a fog in the pew," meaning, as you might suspect, that preaching without conviction results in people without direction. I shudder to think of those times where I was guilty of exactly that. Praise God we've snapped out of that murkiness through a laser focus on inviting all people into a living relationship with Christ. But it's an easy place to go if you're not careful. The church's great obstacle, always a temptation, is the limitation that apathy and confusion bring about.

Sometimes it's great how kids deal with the apathy that church can embody. There was a church where the little boys in particular were known for being especially reverent during the sermon, almost like they were gazing up at heaven. When asked how this happened, one Sunday School teacher explained: "With each batch of new Sunday schoolers, I casually mention that we had to fire the artist who had done the stained glass windows in the sanctuary. I tell them how he put some bad words in the artwork of the ceiling panels, which we didn't discover until after the windows were set in place. Now all the energetic boys who get bored in worship spend their time staring straight up, studying." How many of us do the adult equivalent of that, passing our time looking for profanity in the stained glass?

I look at the landscape of Peter's descendants in the modern church, and I realize that almost all of its limitations come from that toxic brew of apathy, indecision, and even boredom. The gates of Hades do whatever they can to keep us bound up in these limitations. And yet Jesus tells Peter, the other disciples, and us that these gates of Hades will not overcome the church. What is the source of his confidence?

Recall when and where Jesus said these words, and then remember the first rule of real estate: Location, Location, Location! He spoke them in response to Peter's declaration that Jesus is "the Christ, the Son of the living God" (verse 16). And Peter and Jesus both spoke at Caesarea Philippi, with its history of idol worship and sex and Caesar's power. Peter was surrounded by lies when Jesus asked him, "Who do you say that I am?" (verse 15). Peter stood amidst the lies that Baal and Pan are gods, that promiscuity will help the community flourish, that Caesar is the supreme ruler. And in the face of all these lies, Peter declared the truth: Jesus is "the Son of the living God." Jesus is Lord, and these things are not. The promise that Jesus makes in verse 18—"The gates of the underworld won't be able to stand against it"—can't be separated from the proclamation Peter makes in verse 16—"You are the Christ." Hades, the forces of death, will try to limit the church, but Jesus says that the gates of the underworld will not overcome it. And the truth from Peter's mouth is the source of the liberation that Jesus promises!

Here's what I hear Jesus saying to us: ***Truth liberates what apathy limits***.

Apathy, confusion, and frustration are the powers of Hades, and they will limit the church. But the truth that Jesus is Lord breaks us free of those limitations. So often we think the truth is confining or restricting when in fact the opposite is the case. Truth is liberating. The answer to apathy in your own walk with God is not to become busier with church matters. And the answer to apathy in a whole church is not more razzle-dazzle. It's not more tasks, or programs, or spectacles. The answer is truth! The answer is to celebrate the truth that Jesus is Lord. Caesar is not lord; sex is not lord; idols are not lord. Rejoice when people call you weird because you believe this. As Flannery O'Connor, whom you met in Chapter 1, reportedly said, "You shall know the truth, and the truth shall make you odd." Jesus,

DO YOU SPEND TOO MUCH TIME IN ACTIVITY AND TOO LITTLE TIME IN WONDER?

and Jesus alone, is the Son of the living God. Delight in that truth and it will truly set you free. It will make you come alive inside like nothing else can. That is the source of your enthusiasm, your commitment to Christ and the church. Programs and spectacular worship won't do it, no matter how powerful the music, preaching, or prayers. God help me if I ever get bored with proclaiming and explaining the truth that God became a man and defeated the powers of death. God help me if I ever just read that out of a book matter-of-factly and explain it as dry as toast. Jesus is the Son of the living God. *Truth liberates what apathy limits*.

Some of you reading this are in churches where the harder you work, the more listless you become. You organize fundraisers, attend committee meetings, and caravan to conferences. All to little or no avail. Have you considered that you spend too much time in activity and too little time in wonder? The answer to church malaise is not harder work; it's deeper worship! It's allowing yourself to be captured by the sublime beauty of the truths we find in the gospel and in the creeds.

And it's always been this way! The truth liberates, and even the most casual stroll through church history will demonstrate this time and time again. Five centuries ago, the Protestant Reformation helped the church break free from the chains of apathy, ritual, and corruption. That reformation was grounded in the truth of the gospel, that we are saved by grace through faith. The Pentecostal revival centered on Azusa Street in Southern California broke loose from apathetic religion in the early 1900's, with a renewed celebration of the truth that the Holy Spirit still acts powerfully in individuals and churches. That revival in particular is why we at Good Shepherd have monthly healing services. At a Methodist church! Why? Because we are caught up in the wonder that the Holy Spirit is every bit as much alive today as when the apostles preached. A return to the Spirit-inspired truth that Jesus is Lord is vital if churches are to break free from the chains of apathy.

And make no mistake, the truth is old. It is ancient. This is so different from what our culture values. We are taught to esteem the new, the up-and-coming, the innovative, the Next Big Thing. But the truth is not new. The proclamation that Jesus is Lord has been true ever since Peter uttered it in Caesarea Philippi two thousand years ago. The beautiful summary of our faith in the Apostles' Creed lacks a modern feel, but the story it tells remains as powerful as ever:

> I believe in God, the Father Almighty,
>   creator of heaven and earth.
>
> I believe in Jesus Christ, his only Son, our Lord,
>   who was conceived by the Holy Spirit,
>   born of the Virgin Mary,
>   suffered under Pontius Pilate,

was crucified, died, and was buried;
he descended to the dead.
On the third day he rose again;
he ascended into heaven,
is seated at the right hand of the Father,
and will come again to judge the living and the dead.

I believe in the Holy Spirit,
the holy catholic church,
the communion of saints,
the forgiveness of sins,
the resurrection of the body
and the life everlasting. Amen.[2]

At Good Shepherd we don't teach anything new. I often tell the congregation that if I stand up and declare that I have a "new revelation" from the Lord then it is time for them to get another preacher. Through our worship, ministries, and Life Groups we don't proclaim new things. We excavate and celebrate the old, unchanging truths. We may look new, modern, and high-tech. We have a praise band, an excellent audio/visual ministry, and a stellar website. We preach in jeans and post our worship videos online. But the person who thinks we're all tech has it wrong. All of these things are simply vehicles of communication. Through them we pass on a truth that has been true for a long, long time. We may teach with new technology, but the content of our teaching at Good Shepherd is ancient and treasured. We handle it carefully and lovingly; we want it to soar in our lives so that it is not just words on a page (or on a screen) but a beauty that makes us come alive inside.

It's a lot like our favorite music, which for me is the song "The Streets Have No Name," by U2. Seriously, I love that song. It will be played at my funeral. And the first time I heard it, I played the vinyl album on a record player. When I played the record, I heard the sound of my favorite song. Later on, I got a Walkman. I had my headphones and I was stylin'. I got my U2 cassette tape and when I played it in the Walkman, I heard . . . well, the sound of my favorite song. Around the early 2000's, we got iPods. And when I put my U2 music on an iPod and played it digitally, I would still hear the sound of my favorite song. Now, even iPods are yesterday, and many of us have our music directly on our smartphones. And if I play the song on a smartphone, well you get the idea. It's the same great song every time! The delivery system becomes progressively higher-tech through the years, but the song, the content, remains the same. And it's the same with truth that we Christians proclaim and live by. At Good Shepherd Church, the place looks new and our tech is current. But we have an ancient message. We teach an old truth. We treasure our message and strive to communicate it in the most compelling ways possible. We want to be a smartphone church in an era where many still prefer to use phonographs. But the truth doesn't change, and it's not our tech that is the source of our enthusiasm and life. *Truth liberates what apathy limits.*

THE TRUTH IS NOT TAME.

In light of all this, I have to ask you: Where is apathy limiting your personal faith? Do you have a vulnerability to competing faith claims because you've never really considered the decisiveness of Jesus? Are you tempted to regard faith as an activity rather than an animating presence? If you are wrestling with apathy, celebrate truth. Ponder it, meditate upon it, and encourage one another with it. This week, for example, in the daily Scripture readings, I'm giving you a selection of New Testament passages that are unparalleled in their exaltation of Christ: John 1:1-18; Hebrews 1:1-4; Colossians 2:1-23; Philippians 2:5-11; and John 8:21-59. Read them slowly. Then read them out loud. Then write them down. Let those truths seep into your spirit and fill your soul.

It's like the cartoon I saw once, where church leaders from another denomination were competing on a game show called "Name That Trinity." They were coming up with new ways to name the Father, Son, and Holy Spirit in an effort to "update" the ways we speak about God in the church. Eventually, the responses became so absurd that someone suggested "Rock, Paper, Scissors!" No, no, no. Don't mess with that truth. The truth that Jesus is the Son of the living God has never been out of date. The gates of Hades will not overcome it.

There are always forces trying to limit that truth, to keep it gated in Hades—keep it mired in uncertainty, murkiness, and apathy. Those attempts are never-ending, and they can come from inside the church or outside the church. But Jesus promises Peter and the other disciples that "the gates of the underworld won't be able to stand against it." We too can trust that promise now and beyond. We don't need to update the truth, jazz it up, or change it. We can proclaim it boldly, like Peter did in Caesarea Philippi, trusting in Jesus' promise that the truth and the church that proclaims it will prevail. The truth is liberating.

Make no mistake: The truth is not tame. It is neither convenient nor politically correct. Jesus is Lord, which means that Buddha is not. Jesus is Lord, which means heaven and hell are real. Jesus is Lord, which means the kingdom of heaven demands more of your allegiance than the United States of America. Jesus is Lord, which means it matters how you live your life and conduct your relationships: celibacy in singleness and faithfulness in heterosexual marriage. Jesus is Lord, which means that what you do in your bedroom or with your money is his business too, not just yours. Peter's declaration that Jesus is the Messiah, the Son of the living God, is an inconvenient and unpopular truth when you get down to it. It is an odd truth, believed by people who come to delight in their oddity.

At Good Shepherd, we sing a modern worship tune called "This I Believe," by Hillsong. It is essentially the words of the creed put to a rock and roll rhythm. After a recent Sunday in which we sang that song, I received an e-mail from a young woman who is part of our worship team. She thoroughly belongs to the millennial generation and, like some of her peers, she tweets regularly and jokes irreverently. Many religious leaders today will tell you that she and others in her generation believe all truth is relative, and modern Christianity makes a critical mistake if it holds up decisive truth claims. Yet here is the note she sent me:

> Yesterday, while singing with the band, I was empowered with a new love for "This I Believe" because of how defining and declarative the song is. Just one part of a verse and the chorus make the unique claims that separate Christianity from all the other religions of the world. The song makes claims that defeat other religious teachings and define Christianity as the one true faith. When I realized this yesterday, I was overcome with new love and appreciation for this song. Yes, I know it's the creed in song form . . . but it was so much more powerful to me when singing (and declaring) it during worship. These beliefs I'm singing about are the very ones that people died for, and they are the very ones that the Christian faith has held on to when others went astray.

Friends, I can promise you the gates of Hades will never overcome a liberating truth like that.

Questions for Reflection and Discussion

Write responses and other thoughts in the space below each question. If you are discussing the book in a small group, prepare for the meeting by writing answers in advance.

1. Why did Jesus choose Caesarea Philippi to ask his disciples about his identity? What would have been the effect of asking them this question in another location, such as Jerusalem? What other significant places might he have chosen?

2. Why were the Israelites tempted to worship Baal? What other "gods" are you tempted to worship alongside the Lord? Why is this a temptation for you?

3. What does Jesus mean by telling Peter, "Happy are you . . . because no human has shown this to you? Rather my father who is in heaven has shown you" (Matthew 16:17)? What does this say about the nature of Peter's declaration about Jesus?

4. How do you respond to the idea of "absolute truth"? Is there such a thing, or is truth more flexible, so that what's true "for you" might not necessarily be true "for me"? How can we confidently identify what is true and what is not?

5. In what ways are you apathetic, frustrated, jaded, or bored with your faith? What are the "gates of Hades" in your own life that are holding you back?

6. How can the truth that Jesus is Lord set you free from these limitations?

7. What are some markers of an apathetic church? of an apathetic person?

8. What are the most powerful truth claims that compete with Jesus today?

9. How does our faith in Jesus Christ make us odd? How can you or your church become more odd, more counter-cultural, than you already are?

Let the Truth Set You Free

Turn back in this chapter to the page containing the Apostles' Creed, the ancient statement of our Christian faith (pages 61-62). Read it slowly out loud, either by yourself or together with other group members if you are studying this book in a small group. After each of the three sections (God the Father, Jesus Christ the Son, and the Holy Spirit), pause and whisper, "This truth liberates me" before reciting the next section.

Distribute index cards and pens, and have each person copy down the Apostles' Creed on one side of the index card. On the other side write, "This Truth Liberates Me." Each day this week, set aside some time to read the creed slowly. As you read, reflect on how this truth sets you free and what it sets you free from.

Closing Prayer

Eternal God, thank you for the centuries-old good news that Jesus is our Lord and Messiah. May we your people be formed by what is true, even when it is inconvenient and uncomfortable. As we confess that you, Jesus, are the Son of the living God, free us from the prison gates of apathy, frustration, indecision, and boredom. May we be a people filled with life and truth. We come to you, and you alone, for salvation and freedom. Amen.

Daily Scripture Readings

These Scripture passages beautifully proclaim and celebrate the truth that Jesus Christ is Lord. As you read, open your heart and life to the words, and let them lift you up and set you free.

Monday: John 1:1-18
Tuesday: Hebrews 1:1-4
Wednesday: Colossians 2:1-23
Thursday: Philippians 2:5-11
Friday: John 8:21-59

1. From *The Odyssey*, by Homer; Book 11, lines 489-490.

2. The Apostles' Creed, Ecumenical Version, *The United Methodist Hymnal* (Copyright ©1989 by The United Methodist Publishing House); 882.

4

THE
UNFORGIVABLE SIN

But whoever insults the Holy Spirit will never be forgiven. That person is guilty of a sin with consequences that last forever. (Mark 3:29)

Worst. Head scratcher. Ever. The unforgivable sin. Unpardonable. If you commit this sin, there is apparently no turning back. And a lot of people have spent a lot of time scratching their heads over this notion of an unforgivable sin. Some have tried to figure out and define exactly what that eternal sin is. What does it mean to insult the Holy Spirit or, to put it differently, what is blasphemy against the Holy Spirit? Jesus isn't exactly clear on a definition, after all.

Others have tried to figure out if they have ever committed this unforgivable sin without knowing about it. Almost as if they did it unawares, go on to live a good life of faith, and will end up dying and going to hell anyway. What, then, will have been the point of their faithful life? "If I had known I was already lost, I would have just lived it up and sinned away during the rest of my time on earth!" If Jesus didn't clearly tell us what the unforgivable sin was, how can we truly be sure we haven't done it?

Still others, sadly, assume they have committed an unforgivable sin and that it's too late for their souls. I vividly remember a conversation that happened shortly after my own conversion to faith at age seventeen. I was speaking with someone in my grade, excited about my newfound relationship with Christ, trying to get him to consider following Jesus as well. He replied, "Nah, it's too late. I've already done too much." At seventeen. Most of us are just getting started sinning at that point! There was another guy I knew in college, who was headed down a pretty dark path at that time in his life. We were talking about religion and faith and that darkness in his life, and eventually we started talking about hell and the AC/DC song "Highway to Hell." He told me of another AC/DC song called "Hell Ain't a Bad Place to Be," and said, "Maybe that's true. Maybe hell's not such a bad place to be." He figured that was where he was going, and maybe that was all right. Well, hell is a bad place to be. And I always pray that no one hearing my voice or reading my words will end up there.

IT'S ALL ABOUT THE BUILDUP.

As you can see, this one statement from Jesus has led to a lot of head scratching and heart searching. In light of all that, it is important that we figure out what "it" is. We must determine if we can in any sense commit this unforgivable sin—knowingly or unknowingly—and then explore what all this has to do with our lives anyway.

As usual, the answers to these questions come from pulling back from the verse in question to see what is around it. By now, you should be familiar with C.I.E., Context Is Everything. Yes, some of Jesus' sayings don't make sense on their own, but when you see the bigger picture it is often much easier to understand them. And with this head scratcher in particular, it's all about the dialogue, the buildup that precedes Jesus' statement about the unforgivable sin. And in this case, the buildup actually involves Jesus' own family and his religion. Read the larger passage, Mark 3:20-30:

> [20] Jesus entered a house. A crowd gathered again so that it was impossible for him and his followers even to eat. [21] When his family heard what was happening, they came to take control of him. They were saying, "He's out of his mind!"
> [22] The legal experts came down from Jerusalem. Over and over they charged, "He's possessed by Beelzebul. He throws out demons with the authority of the ruler of demons."
> [23] When Jesus called them together he spoke to them in a parable: "How can Satan throw Satan out? [24] A kingdom involved in civil war will collapse. [25] And a house torn apart by divisions will collapse. [26] If Satan rebels against himself and is divided, then he can't endure. He's done for. [27] No one gets into the house of a strong person and steals anything without first tying up the strong person. Only then can the house be burglarized. [28] I assure you that human beings will be forgiven for everything, for all sins and insults of every kind. [29] But whoever insults the Holy Spirit will never be forgiven. That person is guilty of a sin with consequences that last forever." [30] He said this because the legal experts were saying, "He's possessed by an evil spirit."

Look first at verses 20-21. The words "take control" there more literally mean "hold, restrain, or seize." His family wanted to seize him against his will because in their view he was "out of his mind." And if those words conjure up in your mind very sad images of straight jackets, psychiatric wards, and involuntary commitment—think of Jack Nicholson and *One Flew Over the Cuckoo's Nest*—they should. That is what you're supposed to think about here. Something akin to that, if not as dramatic, is what the family wants to do with Jesus. He has a wild popularity and an expanding influence, which they can't understand. So many people are surrounding him that he can't even eat. And for his family, this popularity does more than make them confused; it makes them fearful. So their response is to insult it. To curse it. Throw it to the ground. Jesus' relatives don't have a category for computing this type of power and influence coming from one of their own. They could only dream of having that influence, and so they try to restrain it, seize it, hold it back. Families are tough!

Next up is Jesus' religion. Look at verse 22, where "legal experts" come from Jerusalem and say that Jesus throws out demons with demonic authority. In first-century Judaism, Beelzebul referred to the ruler of demons, or Satan. So the legal experts are saying Jesus has authority from the prince of demons. These experts are some of the religious leaders, and they may have even known Jesus in his childhood. Maybe they were Jesus' childhood preachers, or even his vacation Bible school teachers. And now Jesus is so much more successful than they are; he is able to do the kind of things—religious things—that they can't do. He can cast out demons (Mark 1:21-28), heal people with the touch of his hand (Mark 1:40-45), and draw large crowds to witness his miracles (Mark 3:7-10). So after his family, it's Jesus' religious leaders who respond to him. They see all of Jesus' success, and they are threatened in their role of leadership. So they belittle him and spread lies about him. They say he does what he does by the devil's power, accusing him of being possessed by Beelzebul. Even though he is doing things that are inherently good, they say he does them via a power that is truly evil.

All of this launches Jesus into pointing out the absurdity of their accusation, which he does in verses 23-27. He tells the religious leaders, "A kingdom involved in civil war will collapse. And a house torn apart by divisions will collapse" (verses 24-25). Another way to translate that second part is, "If a house is divided against itself, that house cannot stand" (NIV). Some of you may remember that Abraham Lincoln said that part about "a house divided against itself," which he did in a speech to his Republican colleagues in 1858.[1] But a bigger, yes, better name had already said it. And because it was originally from the mouth of Jesus, it carried remarkable truth and credibility when Lincoln retweeted it eighteen hundred years later. Jesus goes on to say that Satan cannot endure if he fights against himself and that only by tying up a strong adversary can someone burglarize his home (verses 26-27). Jesus is telling the legal experts that their accusations are senseless. They have said that Jesus throws out demons by the ruler of demons, Beelzebul. In response, Jesus shows them how foolish it is to think that Satan would fight against himself. Jesus' miracles are in fact evidence that the demons have already been overcome.

Finally, we come to the head scratcher verses. After showing the legal experts that their accusations are baseless—illogical, even— Jesus continues: "I assure you that human beings will be forgiven for everything, for all sins and insults of every kind. But whoever insults the Holy Spirit will never be forgiven. That person is guilty of a sin with consequences that last forever" (verses 28-29). So this is not just a blanket, universal statement. Jesus introduces the idea of an eternal, unforgivable sin in response to the legal experts who have insulted him by questioning his legitimacy. As if to cement this connection, Mark states it directly in the very next verse: "He said this because the legal experts were saying, 'He's possessed by an evil spirit'" (verse 30). They have called the Holy Spirit an evil spirit, and therefore insulted the very Spirit of God. And Jesus tells them that such an insult will never be forgiven.

There's something deeper going on with the legal experts, an attitude underlying their assertion that Jesus is in league with the devil. It is an attitude they shared with Jesus' family, who said he was "out of his mind" when they tried to seize him (verse 21). In both cases, Jesus' wild success led to insult. Jesus had more success than his family could comprehend and more impact than the religious leaders could tolerate. And so they insulted him. The family envied his influence, lacking any category to understand it, and they cursed him by trying to have him committed. The leaders envied his success, that he could do things they were unable to achieve, and so they cursed him by accusing him of being in league with evil powers.

ENVY IS THE ART OF COUNTING ANOTHER'S BLESSINGS INSTEAD OF YOUR OWN.

More than anything, this story is about envy. Whatever else this story is about, whatever else the unforgivable sin is, envy is swimming around the middle of it. And I suppose that is appropriate. Because I don't think a whole lot has changed about human nature in the last two thousand years. You know what envy is, right? It's not just jealousy. Jealousy is saying, "I want what you have." Envy takes it a step further and says, "I want what you have, *and I don't want you to have it anymore.*" Envy is the art of counting another's blessings instead of your own. Envy is a thief. It takes the image of God we all carry and makes it all but unrecognizable, robbing us of the ability to see the image of God in others and in ourselves. And, as we'll see, it even robs us of the ability to receive God's love.

And it starts when we are so young! Envy seems to be hard-wired into the very fabric of who we are. Take, for example, my daughter, who is now twenty-four years old. Back when she was three years old, she had the run of the house, getting all the attention from both of her parents. But then we played the dirtiest trick you can ever play on a three-year-old: We had another child. We brought home Riley, our son, and it turned three-year-old Taylor's world upside down. She was rocked, turned inside out, because the world no longer revolved around her. All of that family attention and influence was suddenly shared. And when our son was about two months old, we went on a retreat with the church we were then a part of in Monroe, North Carolina. There were probably about fifty people all together in a spacious retreat house. And one morning on the retreat, three-year-old Taylor decided to wake up two-month-old Riley . . . by biting him on the nose. Hard. This was envy with teeth marks! There was shrieking all over that retreat house, and I worried people would think we were raising cannibal children! That is still the most infamous event in the history of our little family, and envy was at the root of it. It starts so, so young.

You may not be at the biting stage anymore, but odds are you still struggle with envy. Perhaps you're envious of a sibling or other family member, who is blessed with influence or success that you don't have. Maybe it's that happy couple you know, who are hard for you to be around because you're still single or in a dead-end relationship. Maybe you envy a coworker, the woman or man who got that promotion instead of you. Taylor must have come by it honestly, because I know I tend to be envious of other preachers—other clergy members who are more influential, better recognized, and more widely published. It is so easy to envy the success of someone else. They have more, accomplish more, dress more, drive more. And you're so busy tallying up all their blessings that you can't possibly count your own.

Where in your life does envy rear its ugly head? Where is it stealing not only your capacity for joy but also your ability to delight in how God blesses other people? Who or what causes you to say, "I want what you have, and I don't want you to have it anymore"? What is the source of your envy, and how does it express itself?

It is in our nature to envy what others have. And we humans have a typical response to those whom we envy: We ridicule them. Sometimes out loud, and sometimes in our own minds, we belittle them to make ourselves feel better. They have something that we cannot attain, so we curse and insult them because really, deep down, we want what they have. That is what happens with Jesus' family, and then again with the legal experts. They see in Jesus a level of success and power that they don't understand and can't have, and they insult him for it. His family says he's out of his mind. The religious leaders say he's possessed by a demon. When someone in our lives has something we want—influence, success, wealth, attention, and so forth—we both desire it and resent it. We want what they have, and we don't want them to have it.

YOU CURSE WHAT YOU ENVY.

Do you see what's going on? You curse what you envy. You ridicule what you cannot attain. This behavior is especially dangerous when the target of our envy is godliness. Some people have a visible, tangible, living relationship with Christ. When you meet such a person, you know immediately that they are deeply connected to God, and it can put your own relationship with Christ in perspective. We recognize their godliness and we know that we are not in that same place, so we ridicule them. We insult their godliness. We question its legitimacy. I remember teaching tennis at a Christian summer camp during my college years. And even among a Christian camp staff there was one young man who stood out because of his spirituality. He was holy. Now, to be holy is to be different. And this guy was different—weird, even. Because of that, other staffers didn't always treat him well. We responded to his holiness, his difference, not with Christian kindness but with Christian cruelty. Finally, I asked the camp director why we—those other guys, not me, because I was just perfect—treated this person so badly. The director responded, "I think his level of holiness intimidates everyone else." He was right. Our peer had deeper connection with God than we did, and our response was to lash out at him.

You could say that Jesus' family and the legal experts envied and cursed Jesus' godliness in Mark 3:20-30. You could argue that at the root, they didn't just envy Jesus' influence and success, but his holiness, his connection to God the Father. But of course it goes beyond even that. Jesus is not just godly; he is God. The religious leaders saw in Jesus a level of success and power that they could not achieve, and they ended up cursing the one they should have been worshiping. They questioned his legitimacy. They called Jesus, the Son of God, a servant of the devil. They cursed what they envied to the point of attributing the work of God to the power of Satan.

That is where envy finally takes us: We curse what we envy and we end up cursing God. We envy and curse that which is unattainable. It starts with other people, but our envy reaches higher and higher and eventually it reaches God. Deep down, at a fundamental level, we want to be God. Some of you reading that last sentence will ask, "How in the world is that true?" And I suggest that the ways in which we want to be God, much like the army of Satan himself, are *legion*:

> We want to be smarter than God, so we rewrite, redefine, or simply ignore some of God's most basic commandments.
>
> We want to be more just and fair than God, so we decide there must be all kinds of paths to eternal life. We make Jesus into a way, a truth, and a life instead of *the* Way, *the* Truth, and *the* Life (see John 14:6).
>
> We want to be more powerful than God, so we glibly declare that God is completely uninvolved in the way weather works and disasters happen.

We long to be God, and when we realize we're not, we end up hating God. If you're not convinced, remember the man and the woman in the garden of Eden. You know, that story way back at the beginning of the Bible that tells us how this whole mess got started, which also uncovers human nature in a starkly honest way (Genesis 2:4–3:24). What was it that the tempter, the serpent, used to trick the man and the woman into eating the forbidden fruit in the garden? Envy! He introduced them to the possibility of being like God: "God knows that on the day you eat from it, you will see clearly and you will be like God, knowing good and evil" (Genesis 3:5). The serpent planted a seed of envy that caused the first humans to disobey their Creator, each of them eating from the tree of the knowledge of good and evil out of their desire to be like God. And look at the chaos that has ensued as a result of their disobedience.

But we can go back even further than the Garden, even before the creation of the world we live in. Second Peter tells us this: "God didn't spare the angels when they sinned but cast them into the lowest level of the underworld and committed them to chains of darkness, keeping them there until the judgment" (2 Peter 2:4). Our Christian tradition has long understood this verse as a reference to Satan, meaning that he was first created as an angel and fell from grace when he rebelled against God. What was it that made Satan himself, the former angel, fall into rebellion? Envy! He wanted what God had. He wanted the prestige, the acclaim, the praise! He longed for it for himself and couldn't stand to see it going to another. Envy is a demonic thief and it has been that way from the beginning. I think that's why Jesus himself said, "The thief enters only to steal, kill, and destroy" (John 10:10).

THE UNFORGIVABLE SIN IS NOT SOMETHING YOU DO. IT'S AN ATTITUDE YOU HAVE.

So now it's clear. This envy stretches back before creation. It shows up at the dawn of creation. It rears its head in Mark 3 among Jesus' family and religious leaders. And it lands squarely in our lives today, among the people of Good Shepherd Church and those reading this book. You curse what you envy. Envy robs you of your humanity and blinds you to the spark of divinity in others. And eventually, because there is nothing and no one higher, you envy God. We want to be like God, and we realize that we aren't God. Then we hate God. And that is unforgivable.

See, the unforgivable sin is not something you do. It's an attitude you have. It's not an act you commit. It's a journey you take. And it becomes a journey that takes you. It's this all-consuming, uncontrollable thievery, and it starts so young. And mark my words: It begins with people. It starts with people, and if you don't check it, this desire and this resentment will grow and grow until God finally becomes the target of your envy. Your heart becomes corroded like a car battery, covered in bitterness and hatred of God, insulated against God's love and forgiveness. God doesn't break through a corroded heart, because such a heart curses God and turns away from divine love. Envy steals, and taken to its ultimate end, it will rob you even of your salvation. The unforgivable sin is not an action. It's a journey. And I don't want any of you to take even the first step.

I once heard something very wise in an open meeting of Alcoholics Anonymous: "If you get hit by a train, it's not the

CELEBRATION RESTORES WHAT ENVY STEALS.

caboose that kills you." The deadly part is the engine and cars at the front. The same is true for our envy. That corrosive journey starts somewhere—siblings, coworkers, the rich and famous, other preachers—and it ends nowhere: eternal separation from God. Envy is a master thief, and it will steal you away to an unforgivable place. Have you started on this journey? How far have you gone down the path of envy? How can you turn around and find a better road?

I long for something better for you and me. I want us not to curse what is beyond us, but to celebrate what is good in others. I want us to celebrate the blessings in our neighbors' lives, not insult them for it. I want us to be able to step back and see how the success, the blessings, the godliness of others elevates the whole enterprise. For my part, I want to look at other pastors who are successful, influential, well-known, and not dismiss them as phony and inauthentic. I want to be able to say, "Thank God. The Kingdom is advancing and the King is still on his throne."

Here's what I know from experience and study to be true; here is what I think Jesus is driving at in Mark 3: *Celebration restores what envy steals.*

I want my hearers and readers to stop resenting the success of others and to start recognizing how the blessings of one benefit all. While envy hollows us out, celebration fills us up—it fills us up with gratitude for God's power and appreciation for God's people. And as a side benefit, we stop wasting so much time and energy being jealous of others and start devoting our minds and spirits to crafting our own successes! *Celebration restores what envy steals.*

Speaking of celebration, a great band doesn't sound great because they're all playing the same instrument, but because they are all adding their part to the whole sound. It wouldn't do much good for us to have six guitars competing with one anther. In the same way, a great choir doesn't sound great because they're all singing the same part; they sound great because each member is singing a part of the harmony that makes up the song.

Neil Armstrong is another great example. He was the first person to walk on the moon, and we all know what he got to say: "One small step for man, one giant leap for mankind." Guess what?

He didn't do it alone. It took over two hundred thousand people to get him there! That's right, more than two hundred thousand engineers, scientists, truck drivers, painters, carpenters, and secretaries, all putting aside ego and envy for the sake of a cause much larger than themselves. They could have either cursed Neil Armstrong for his fame or celebrated what they all accomplished together. A lot of smart people worked on that project, and I'm quite sure that among them a whole lot of egos were put aside to make one person the first one on the moon. And when those egos were laid aside, it was possible for everyone to delight in the work of others. Don't curse what is beyond you. Celebrate what is within you and those around you. Because *celebration restores what envy steals.*

This week, I have a homework assignment for you. When you start counting up the blessings of others, stop. When you start to pull out that mental calculator, recognize what you're doing and turn it off. And then turn on the calculator you use to add up your own blessings.

Because wouldn't it be great, wouldn't it be marvelous if instead of spending so much time cursing what we envy, we were able to celebrate that God is good? And God is good not only in my life, but in the lives of other people as well. Wouldn't it be life-changing if we gathered on Sunday mornings as the people who spend the week delighting in the goodness of God they see in others? Because who knows? Along the way, you might just save your soul.

Questions for Reflection and Discussion

Write responses and other thoughts in the space below each question. If you are discussing the book in a small group, prepare for the meeting by writing answers in advance.

1. What comes to mind when you hear the phrase, the unforgivable sin? Have you ever worried about committing it? What is an unforgivable sin for you? What would you have a hard time forgiving in somebody else? How does this compare with the unforgivable sin that Jesus mentions in Mark 3:29?

2. Is the idea of a sin that "will never be forgiven" consistent with our Christian faith? Why or why not? How does the explanation of the unforgivable sin in this chapter help you wrestle with this question?

3. Based on Mark 3:20-21, how would you summarize Jesus' relationship with his own family? What do you think is behind their situation? How would you have responded if Jesus had been your brother or son?

4. Think of someone of whom you are envious. What are they like? What is it that you envy about them? When have you been the object of someone else's envy?

5. Take some time and make a mental list of the things you envy most in others. If you wish, write the list down. Spend a few minutes reflecting on your list. What does your envy say about you or about what you value?

6. How does envy affect your relationship with other people, especially those you envy? How does it affect your relationship with Jesus?

7. In what ways are you envious of God?

8. This chapter drew a connection between envy of others and envy of God. How far have you gone down the path of envy? How can you turn around and find a better road?

9. Think of a time you have celebrated the blessings and gifts you saw in another rather than becoming envious. Why were you able to do this, and what was the result? What can you do to adopt this attitude of celebration more often?

Count Your Own Blessings

In a notebook, on a piece of paper, or on your phone, make a list of how God has blessed you. As you write each item down, whisper a short prayer of thanks. Review the list for a few minutes each day this week, adding other blessings as you think of them. Whenever you find yourself counting the blessings of others, turn your mind to your own blessings instead. Then praise God for the good you see in those around you as well.

If you are studying this series in a group, share your lists of blessings with each other. Thank God for your own blessings, and also for the good things that have happened for your fellow group members.

Closing Prayer

God, deliver us from envy. We know that envy comes from a single-minded focus on ourselves, and it causes us to curse others and you. We thank you that you are able to intervene in our lives and turn our hearts from the path of envy. Heal us so that we might praise your goodness. Give us eyes to see our own blessings and be grateful, and to celebrate the good things we see in others. All for your glory. Amen.

Daily Scripture Readings

Monday: 2 Corinthians 5:11-6:2
Tuesday: Luke 15:11-32
Wednesday: Matthew 12:25-30; Luke 11:17-22
Thursday: 1 Corinthians 13:4-13
Friday: Revelation 20:11-15

1. The text of the speech can be accessed at *www.pbs.org/wgbh/aia/part4/4h2934t.html*. Accessed 27 March 2015.

5

LET THE DEAD BURY THEIR OWN DEAD

Another man, one of his disciples, said to him, "Lord, first let me go and bury my father." But Jesus said to him, "Follow me, and let the dead bury their own dead. (Matthew 8:21-22)

Note: This was sermon was originally delivered at Good Shepherd United Methodist Church in 2011 as part of a series called Jesus Tweets.

Now what I am getting ready to say may well strike you as odd, but here goes: Funerals are a big deal for me and for the church I serve. Anyone who knows me is aware that I take funerals and memorial services very seriously; if one happens at Good Shepherd (as opposed to a funeral home), everything else around the church pretty much stops. Other things we have going on at the church grind to a halt, and our staff and volunteers go all in. From our facilities to our music to our food to our message, we strive to put our very best out there for funeral and memorial services. I expect that of myself, and I expect it of our team at Good Shepherd. By now, I think, it has even gotten to the point where the people of the church expect that kind of full-service experience. When people are grieving, we want to give them the best we have to offer. It is the kind of urgent ministry I think is vital, and I want Good Shepherd actually to be known for it. I want good funerals to be part of our reputation.

This all came home to me back in November of 2006 when my father, who was then ninety-five, was dying in Austin, Texas. I got a phone call that it would happen soon, a matter of days or perhaps even hours, so I flew down to Austin as quickly as I could. As soon as I walked in the front door of my parents' house, I was surrounded by my brothers and sisters (all of whom are much older and not nearly as good looking). They were all asking, "You'll do the funeral, right? You've got to. You'll give the eulogy?" Mind you, our father hadn't even died yet. But I had all of my older siblings—all six of them—right in front of me giving me a tremendous amount of both pressure and affirmation. I felt the heavy weight of their expectations, and there really wasn't much of a choice in the matter. (As I said in Chapter 2, that's an extra benefit of having a pastor in the family!) I led the service when my father did pass away, and everything went well. But in those days, it was as if time stopped for me. It really was like everything else in my life shut down. It didn't matter what was going on back in Charlotte with the church. The most important thing for me and for my family was gathering, grieving, and in my case preparing and delivering a eulogy. That's what was expected, and it's what I did. Our congregational priority of good funerals became a personal mandate.

So you can imagine my surprise, my discomfort, my *objection*, whenever I read this statement from Jesus: "Follow me, and let the dead bury their own dead" (Matthew 8:22). Wow. This might just be the most insensitive thing he ever said. A would-be follower has asked Jesus, "Lord, first let me go and bury my father" (verse 21). And Jesus responds not with compassion, not with understanding or heartache. He bluntly orders, "Follow me, and let the dead bury their own dead." Not only is this response terribly insensitive, it has to do with this close-to-my-heart subject of funerals and grieving.

This is when the head scratching turns heartbreaking and even spirit-quenching.

CONTEXT IS STILL EVERYTHING.

To resolve not only this biblical dilemma but even my personal objection, we're going to make sense of this verse by, of course, diving into the surrounding verses first. Because, as you well know, Context Is Everything. These verses, Matthew 8:18-22, will show us the larger issues that come into play as Jesus addresses those who wish to follow him:

> [18] Now when Jesus saw the crowd, he ordered his disciples to go over to the other side of the lake. [19] A legal expert came and said to him, "Teacher, I'll follow you wherever you go."
> [20] Jesus replied, "Foxes have dens, and the birds in the sky have nests, but the Human One has no place to lay his head."
> [21] Another man, one of his disciples, said to him, "Lord, first let me go and bury my father."
> [22] But Jesus said to him, "Follow me, and let the dead bury their own dead."

In these verses of Matthew 8, two men approach Jesus with a desire to follow him. Jesus first rebuffs the application of a legal expert who says to him, "Teacher, I'll follow you wherever you go" (verse 19). In response, Jesus tells him that "foxes have dens and the birds in the sky have nests, but the Human One has no place to lay his head" (verse 20). What an odd answer! The irony there, of course, is that Jesus is the Creator, and the Creator has no permanent place within his creation. But that is another sermon for another day. Because we're concerned with the following verse, 8:21, where this little scene takes a turn for the worst as someone says, "first let me go and bury my father." Look above and read the first part of verse 21 again carefully. Notice anything? The man who speaks to Jesus is *already a disciple*. That little detail is not by accident. Matthew wants us to know that this man has already made a decision to follow Jesus and has acted on it. He is in. He takes Communion. He served a stint on the trustees. He's been on a mission trip. He tithes. He is even studying HEAD SCRATCHERS with his Sunday school class! This man is one of Jesus' disciples, and he faces a situation like I faced in Austin in 2006: His father is dead, and he's needed at a funeral. I suspect that for him, time has stopped.

In first-century Judaism, the obligation of children to tend to their parents' funeral was a religious responsibility of the utmost importance. It superseded many other important Jewish observances outlined in the Law of Moses. If you had to choose between studying Torah at the synagogue and a funeral, choose the funeral. Between attending a festival meal and a funeral, choose the funeral. All those expectations were heightened if you were the son of a father who had just died. Why? It was a practical, poignant way for the Jews of that time to live out the fifth of the Ten Commandments, "honor your father and your mother" (Exodus 20:12). It was your duty as a child, especially if you were a son, to see to the proper burial of your father. And if you were in the middle of it, time stopped. This man had the burden of expectations upon him—the expectations of his family, his society, and his entire religion on him. It was expected that he would bury his father promptly and properly.

But what was not expected—nor was it sensitive or caring—was the reply Jesus gave in verse 22: "Follow me, and let the dead bury their own dead." The statement started off appropriately enough. Jesus began by saying, "Follow me, . . ." which is all right because he was after all talking to a would-be follower. That part makes sense, and he could have said any number of good things next. If Jesus had asked me for some pastoral advice here, I would have had some suggestions for what he could tell this grieving disciple with so many expectations upon him:

> *Follow me . . . and we'll go through this together.*
> *Follow me . . . and I will help you do and say all the right things as you pay respects to your father.*
> *Follow me . . . and we'll make sure nobody is disappointed.*
> *Follow me . . . and we'll give your dad a sendoff to remember.*
> *Follow me . . . and I'll even help you prepare your dad's eulogy.*

Of course, none of those excellent statements flowed from Jesus' mouth. Evidently, he's doing just fine ruling the universe on his own and doesn't want my advice. Because what came after "follow me" were the awful words: *Let the dead buy their own dead.* Unthinkable words. This man came to Jesus with a perfectly legitimate desire to follow the obligations of his day and grieve properly for his dead father. And Jesus told him to let the dead bury their own dead. I guarantee everyone who overheard that exchange was left with their mouths agape and their spirits shaken.

THE SCANDAL IS THE POINT.

And for years—centuries, really—people have tried to get around the scandal of these words. Pastors and theologians have interpreted them in ways that soften them, making them more palatable for our ears and eyes. One approach suggests that the man's father wasn't really dead yet, but he was old and would die soon. The follower was really asking permission to spend the last

FOLLOWERS ABANDON WHAT'S EXPECTED TO EMBRACE WHAT'S ETERNAL.

several months with his father, holding onto that elusive quality time and getting his affairs in order before he actually passed. A second interpretation says that the father had really been dead for some time, long enough for the body to have decayed, meaning it was time to transfer his father's bones to a bone box. Secondary burial in a bone box, or ossuary, was a common practice for Jews in the first century A.D., so this interpretation fits with what we know of life in Jesus' day. A third interpretation says that Jesus' words had nothing to do with a funeral at all. In this view, he was merely saying something about the spiritual condition of the people who are in this man's life back home. They were spiritually dead, and Jesus was telling him to leave behind that old life and embrace a new life of following him.

All three of those interpretations draw on a close reading of the text with attention to the history of Jesus' own time period. But these readings, and others I haven't mentioned, have the effect of robbing the words of their power and stripping them of their scandal. These interpretations make Jesus a little more comfortable, a little safer for us to be around.

But know this: The scandal is the point! Stark insensitivity is the purpose behind Jesus' words. The man—already a disciple—makes a reasonable request: Let me do what is expected, acceptable, and even right. And Jesus says in reply that if he's going to follow him— really follow him—then his priorities will have to change. He will have to cast off old things and follow Jesus single-mindedly. He will have to be willing to disappoint some people, perhaps even himself, and jettison expectations. Jesus is telling this man that following him will come with a heavy cost. His words are shocking and insensitive . . . and brilliant. Let the dead bury their own dead. Jesus is not into playing games; he doesn't want to be at the periphery of our lives.

What I hear Jesus saying is this: ***Followers abandon what's expected to embrace what's eternal.***

We all have heavy expectations that have been placed upon us—by our friends, our family, our society, even by our church. And Jesus says that if we want to follow him, we need to abandon those expectations to do so wholeheartedly. Jesus probably does want us to attend our own parents' funeral; I don't believe I sinned or betrayed Jesus by dropping everything for a while to head to Austin in 2006. But he wants to be sure that he is the top priority in our lives, that nothing gets in our way as we follow him. For a lot of us, the expectations placed on us by society, family, religion, and self can hinder us from serving Jesus purely and with focus. Many of those expectations are neither bad nor sinful (though some are), but they keep us from becoming the kind of devoted, no-turning-back followers Jesus calls us to be. On so many levels, we let all those expectations from ourselves or others distract us from a living relationship with Jesus Christ.

For some people, it is the expectation to be dating someone. You want to be able to change that Facebook status from "single" to "in a relationship." Perhaps you're putting a lot of energy into dating, finding someone to be with, and it's more about your own "attached" status than any particular person you like. Society places upon you an expectation that being single is undesirable, and you place an expectation on

yourself that you can't be happy unless you're with someone.
Or perhaps you are already in a dating relationship, and the
expectation is for you to stay in it. It is unhealthy and you
know you've compromised, but you don't want the stigma of
being unattached. All your friends are dating or married. What
will people say if you're not with someone? So even though it's
not great, it's probably not even right, you're still hanging on.
You know what? Let the dead bury their own dead! *Followers
abandon what's expected to embrace what's eternal.*

For others, the expectation is a nest egg or retirement plan.
Perhaps you have a preoccupation with your 401(k) or your
savings account. You are expected to build up that account;
you have a strategy for retirement that you expect yourself to
maintain, and those expectations keep you from the kind of
biblical generosity to which you are called. Any time you get
close to taking a major step forward, that expectation cries
out, "Wait, wait, wait!" You step back and return to those
expectations. You know what? Let the dead bury their own dead!

For still others, the expectations center on child rearing.
I know there are a lot of parents out there who are—dare I say
it?—a bit neurotic. They are just a little too obsessed with their
child or children. Their households revolve around their children,
and they see their role as protecting them from danger rather
than exposing them to life. So many parents spend so much time
tending to their children's snacks, or sports, or school, that they
have no time or energy left over to tend to their own spirits.
They become such good parents that they're not good Christians
anymore! And it's all about expectations: The other kids are doing
it; the other parents are doing it; your mom and dad did it so now
you're doing it too. It is what's expected. You know what? Let the
dead bury their own dead! *Followers abandon what's expected to
embrace what's eternal.*

Others out there are still on an endless quest to gain their
parents' approval. It costs them their self-respect at times
and harms their marriage at others, but they feel a burden of
expectations to please and impress. Affirmation their parents

reluctantly gave when they were kids seems within their grasp if they just bow low enough now. You know what? Let the dead bury their own dead! *Followers abandon what's expected to embrace what's eternal.*

GOD PUT YOU HERE TO PURSUE THE KINGDOM.

It is all about a decision to stop pleasing people and start pursuing the kingdom of heaven. With focus. It's like what happened at a baseball game once, when Hank Aaron was up to bat and Yogi Berra was behind him as the catcher. One of Yogi Berra's defining characteristics was his prolific use of words. He talked constantly, and when Hank Aaron was at the plate he started in about how Hank was holding the bat. "Hank," he said, "you're holding the bat wrong. The writing on it should be facing you. You better check it!" Aaron didn't say a word. First pitch: ball one. Yogi kept talking, telling Hank he needed to be able to read the writing on the bat. Otherwise he was holding it wrong. Second pitch: strike one. Yogi kept going, "Hank, check that writing! It needs to face you or you're holding the bat all wrong! You gotta be able to read it!" Next pitch: BOOM! Over the center field wall. One of 755 steroid-free home runs. Aaron went on his home run trot, stepped on home plate, and headed toward the dugout. Then he stopped, looked back at Berra and said simply, *"I didn't come here to read."* Hank knew why he was on the baseball field, and he wasn't going to let chatter distract him. He wasn't there to read. And God didn't put you here to please people. God didn't put you here to pursue expectations that others put on you or that you put on yourself. God put you here to pursue the kingdom single-mindedly. *Followers abandon what's expected to embrace what's eternal.*

When Good Shepherd was launched in the early 1990's, it could easily have been expected to bear all the trappings of a typical United Methodist church: robes, hymnals, organs, and frequent pastoral moves. Yet the church's founding pastor, Claude Kayler, knew something novel for that era: Expected was no longer effective in reaching new generations for Christ. So from its inception, the church has used modern music, casual dress, and imagery from pop culture as a way of inviting all people into a living relationship with Jesus Christ. What's more, the people of the church passionately believe that the gifts of the Holy Spirit are still in operation—and that's why we hold healing services, why we pray over the seats each Sunday morning, and why many in our community pray in tongues. We believe that the combination of cultural savvy and Spirit-fullness is at the heart of what it means to follow in the footsteps of John Wesley . . . even though we hardly look like your typical United Methodist congregation.

And our reach extends well beyond our unique corner in Charlotte . . . as do the implications of this chapter's bottom line. Several years ago, I took a trip to south Asia where I met a Cambodian pastor who leads a church made up largely of former Buddhists. As he prepares the people of that church for baptism, he has the candidates do something significant, painful, and brilliant: They physically have to cut off any token or amulet of their former faith. They have to cut it off and cast it away, knowing their families will be disappointed and may even disown them. It is painful, but it's what they've got to do to be baptized into the Christian faith. The dead trinkets from a dead religion are dead and gone, and they waste no time or energy caring for them and managing the expectations that surround them. Following Jesus is not necessarily for the faint of heart. It requires that we leave something behind, and it may well be something we love. *Followers abandon what's expected to embrace what's eternal.*

You know what I can't get away from here? Jesus says these scandalous words *to a disciple.* He says them to someone who is already a follower! Which brings us some tough news: Following Jesus is hard, and it gets harder through the years, not easier. How's that for a sales pitch?! Follow Jesus and life gets harder. And then after it gets harder, it gets harder still! But as I was writing these words, I was overcome with a prayer:

> Lord, let there be revival through hard words. Don't fill us with false promises of prosperity, but enliven us through truth. Let new life break out among your people and your churches not because of wine and roses but because of blood, sweat, and tears.

I pray that people will cast off good things (career paths, nest eggs) for the sake of better things, spiritual things.

It's like the pastor who asked a group of people: "Do you want to live for the titles or the testimonies? Do you want people to talk about all your accomplishments, or your influence in their lives?" These are two different goals. Do you want the focus to be on you, or to be on how you witness to God's love to those around you? I hope that you focus on the latter, rejecting expectations and pursuing the kingdom of heaven. Because you can be sure of this: Even though following Jesus is hard and it gets harder, it will be worth it. When you embrace your calling and follow Jesus with single-minded devotion, you will be rewarded. When you read the Word, gather with other Christians, pray and fast authentically, and serve the least and the last, you can be sure you are doing something truly important. Don't get me wrong: You won't love every minute. But it is always right and will always be worthwhile. You may disappoint some people you care about along the way; you may frustrate their expectations and let them down. But when it's for the sake of the One who loved you first, there are no regrets. *Followers abandon what's expected to embrace what's eternal.*

We can't avoid the urgency of Jesus' words here in Matthew Chapter 8. It probably wouldn't take long for the disciple to bury his father. Jewish law held that burial should take place on the same day someone died. It wouldn't cause much of a delay in following Jesus. But Jesus' response tells us it's not good enough to plan on following him tomorrow, or next week. The matter is urgent; it's right now. There's such a clear *today* focus in Matthew 8:21-22. I pray that we will have a similar right-this-minute focus, responding to Jesus' call with urgency and abandon. Some of you have never followed Jesus, and today is the day it starts. Others of you have followed Jesus—sort of—but you know something needs to be abandoned for your following to be real. And chances are you know exactly what that something is. What is it that you need to abandon? What expectations do you need to cast off? It could be that unhealthy relationship, that computer usage, that alcohol use or abuse, that overly conservative approach to money, even that continuing fascination with other religions. Whatever it is, cut it off. Leave it behind. Today. Now. Let the dead bury their own dead.

TODAY IS THE DAY IT STARTS.

Do you know what interests me the most about this story in Matthew 8:18-22? We don't know how the man responded to Jesus. We don't know if he went to bury his father or not. Matthew leaves it open-ended. This type of an ending—leaving the story unfinished and unresolved—is actually pretty typical of the Bible. It's a way of letting *us* finish the story. It leaves the ending up to us, putting the resolution in our laps. Matthew is asking us how we will finish that story for ourselves. Will we abandon the expectations that burden us so that we can follow Christ, or will we hold onto them and keep saying, "maybe tomorrow or next week"?

So what of it? How are you going to finish the disciple's story in Matthew 8:18-22? Because it's your story too. Are you going to spend time burying and tending to what's dead, or will you abandon roles and expectations for the urgent call to drop everything and follow Jesus?

Questions for Reflection and Discussion

Write responses and other thoughts in the space below each question. If you are discussing the book in a small group, prepare for the meeting by writing answers in advance.

1. What are some expectations that were placed on you by your family while you were growing up?

2. What additional expectations does our society place on you? What about your church?

3. How do these expectations impede the advance of the gospel in your life?

4. Do any expectations you have to fulfill help advance the gospel in your life? How so?

5. What is your initial response to Jesus' harsh words in Matthew 8:21-22?

6. What will you have to abandon to follow Jesus with more authenticity?

7. Fill in the blank: Jesus, I will follow you wherever you go. But first let me _____.

8. How will you finish the story of Matthew 8:18-22?

Abandon What's Expected

Spend a few minutes thinking through all the expectations that people have of you, including expectations you have of yourself. These expectations can come from your spouse, child, employer, parents, fellow citizens, your church, and so forth.

Take a three-by-five card, and on one side list all of these expectations. Be as specific as you wish.

On the other side of the index card, simply write "Jesus."

Each day this week, examine the card on both sides. As you read it, recognize how following Jesus will influence your response to the other expectations. Will you fulfill them because doing so is a way to be faithful to Jesus? Will you undertake them differently than you would otherwise? Will you have to abandon them altogether? Then make a decision: Which side will you leave "face up" throughout the day? Which side of the card will be your highest priority?

Closing Prayer

Eternal God, help us to follow you with an urgency that prevents us from waiting till tomorrow. Help us to put you before any expectations that others place on us or that we place on ourselves. Give us courage and strength to devote ourselves to you with single-minded focus, abandoning anything that might become a distraction. Give us wisdom to remember that our first calling is to be your disciple. In Jesus' name, amen.

Daily Scripture Readings

Monday: Philippians 1:1-30
Tuesday: Philippians 2:1-30
Wednesday: Philippians 3:1-21
Thursday: Philippians 4:1-23
Friday: Colossians 1:1-29

Other Studies
by Talbot Davis

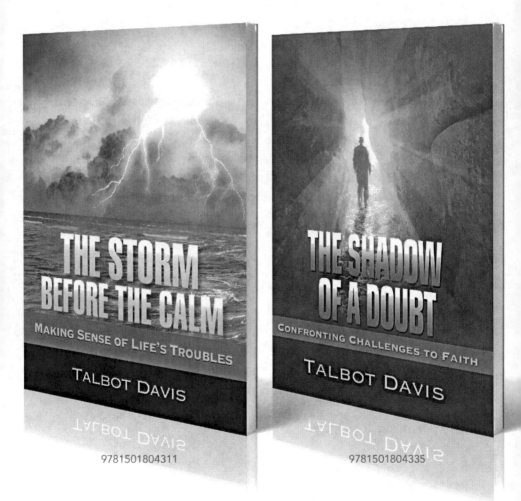

9781501804311

9781501804335

Order your copies today and continue studying with Davis.

Published by

Where will your journey take you next?

CONVERGE
Bible Studies—
where topics and Scriptures merge,
transforming Christian lives.

9781426795534   9781426789533   9781426771576

Visit your local book retailer to see the complete list of Converge Bible Studies.

Published by

Abingdon Press